DANCE, MOVEMENT, AND NUTRITION

Fitness Minutes for a Healthier Life

by

Helene Andreu

Bloomington, IN   authorHOUSE™   Milton Keynes, UK

AuthorHouse™
1663 Liberty Drive, Suite 200
Bloomington, IN 47403
www.authorhouse.com
Phone: 1-800-839-8640

AuthorHouse™ UK Ltd.
500 Avebury Boulevard
Central Milton Keynes, MK9 2BE
www.authorhouse.co.uk
Phone: 08001974150

First published by AuthorHouse 8/7/2006

ISBN: 1-4259-2758-0 (sc)

Library of Congress Control Number: 2006902576

Printed in the United States of America
Bloomington, Indiana

This book is printed on acid-free paper.

PREFACE

Fitness is in. It's everywhere: Fitness Starts Young; Fitness After Forty; Fitness For Life; Buy this machine and stay fit; Join that club and be fit. Try this diet, try that diet, don't quit, stay on it and be fit.

That's all well and good, but DANCE, MOVEMENT, AND NUTRITION - Fitness Minutes for a Healthier Life gets right to the point: a little bit of effort on a daily basis really makes a difference. These fitness minutes take only a short time out of each 24 hours; they probably fit into everyone's schedule. Now if you want to repeat and reread them a few times during the day, or stretch them out by doing two or more workouts, that's your prerogative. But you don't have to; just sticking to the daily 15 or so minutes a day will do wonders. You'll become more aware of your physical self – posture, weight, balance, and nutritional requirements. Your energy level and heart fitness will increase. You'll relax more easily and all aspects of life will take on a rosier glow because you'll feel better.

The movements in DANCE, MOVEMENT, AND NUTRITION - Fitness Minutes for a Healthier Life are fun to do. The numerous photographs throughout the book are a visual enhancement. As you finish one chapter, learn it, practice it, and know it, you'll look forward to seeing what is in the next one. Why? Because the 13 chapters of exercises and dance-like movements are varied, easy to read and do, and engaging. They get at all the areas most people want to tone up: abdomen, hips and buttocks, as well as all the other areas that are either neglected or taken for granted – the neck, hands, arms, pectorals, ankles and calves.

Throughout the book you are provided with hints galore on healthy foods and on nutrition. No other book resembles it, as far as I know. None has a variety of short workouts together with suggestions on healthy, correct calorie consumption. I don't believe I need to press the point that many of us can benefit from short daily workouts to suit our lifestyles, or from being reminded of the importance of blending proper food consumption with sufficient energy output for a long and healthy life.

I wish to thank my family and friends for their encouragement, especially Mary Casmus and Joseph Kress for proofing the original manuscript, and my sister Denise for her help with the layout and final proofing. The photographs of Moses Adebayo, Denise Andreu, Helene Andreu, Samuel Baptiste, Elizabeth Barrow, Yvonne S. Bradshaw, Ramona Brito, Candy Cat, Claudia Charles, Mei G. Chen, Sandra A. Collado, Cassendra Dume, Yensy A. Fernandez, Natiesha Francois, Carmilyn Hall, Alissar Harb, Christina Hardin, Diosys Jose, Mandeep Kaur, Olesya Khanas, Li Qing Kong, Joseph Kress, Jung-Hung Ku, Denise Lugo, Roosevelt E. Martinez, Carline Merizier, Chiranjib Nath, Maria Orozco, Vasilios Pippis, Gabriela Proana, Benancia Rivera, Matilde Rodriguez, Yesenia Rosa, Jacqueline Smith, Blanca Tirado, Kyedi P. Thomas, Yeny Vargas, Hansel Vasquez, Kendra Waithe, and Ru Bing Yang, are by Clotilde, Enia and H. Andreu. I appreciate my students' obvious enjoyment of dance and movement and thank my students at Stuyvesant High School Adult Continuing Education School and at New York City College of Technology, and David Cory, Director of Small World Studios, for permission to take photographs.

TABLE OF CONTENTS

INTRODUCTION

DANCE, MOVEMENT, AND NUTRITION - Fitness Minutes for a Healthier Life. We all have a few minutes a day to spare, especially when it's a question of staying fit for life. In fact, 10 to 20 minutes may not seem like a sufficient amount of time, but you'd be surprised at the difference they can make to your body. Just a few minutes a day of movement, dance and reading and thinking about proper nutrition can certainly become a habitual occurrence even for the busiest schedules. This book is the answer to that frequent question, "How do you expect me to find the time for exercise with my schedule?" When you get used to listening to your body's needs you may find that you'll want to lengthen your fitness session to 1/2 hour or one hour on some days, while on others you may want to do two or more very short sessions. That's all fine, because it's the daily occurrence of these minutes, on a habitual basis that makes for total fitness – toning, strengthening, relaxing, better muscle balance, and increased cardiovascular fitness. And it's the thought, plan, and follow-through given to your meals and snacks that leads to healthier nutrition. As you proceed with your fitness minutes, you'll discover that you really want to spend more than just 10 to 20 minutes; fine – do so whenever you can; 1/2 to 3/4 hour a day would certainly be even better for you.

You'll enjoy **DANCE, MOVEMENT, AND NUTRITION** because it's easy to use. The descriptions are clear to follow; the photographs help too. If you're curious about the dance routines, try one and see how much fun they are.

A great range of movement is covered in the sequences and short dance routines in this book; experts have long advocated this as being the best way to stay fit without boredom. Your muscles will not get in a rut since you won't be doing the same movements all the time. Each of the workouts presented in **DANCE, MOVEMENT, AND NUTRITION** is different. Each consists of five or six sequences that are to be executed slowly, at first, to warm up, then repeated several times and reversed so that the right and left sides get an equal workout. Following this workout comes a short dance routine. You should walk through it a few times, then run or walk through the routine again countless times, but at a snappier, more energetic tempo. Next repeat one or two of the earlier movements slowly and carefully, to cool down at the end of your workout. You decide which movements to do. If you proceed at a continuous pace, you should get it all done in 15 minutes, maybe less.

At the end of many of the movements you'll find notes giving you pointers on better performance, or an alternative way of doing the sequence, perhaps later on, when you are quite familiar with the original workout and are going through the book for the second or third time. Scattered throughout each chapter you'll find a variety of Fitness Minutes – hints on breathing for relaxation, alleviating stress, cross-training, practicing with children, alignment, balance, visualization, etc., as well as Nutrition Hints. The movement sequences include a challenging mixture, not just one type of movement, but some calisthenics for strengthening, some stretches for flexibility, as well as several movements for better balance and alignment, and many for flow and coordination, especially toward the end of the book when you'll have become more proficient.

When you start **DANCE, MOVEMENT, AND NUTRITION - Fitness Minutes for a Healthier Life** you should stick to Chapter One for one week. Read it completely, including the Movement and Nutrition hints interspersed throughout that chapter, before doing the exercises; then do them. Repeat this for several days until you feel confident about the material in the chapter. You'll be able to get through it and remember all the movements easily by the end of week one. The next week, do Chapter One again either slowly for more accuracy and strength, or at a faster pace for more cardiovascular fitness, or go through it two or three times in a row for greater stamina and endurance, then do the cooling down movements. Proceed to the next chapter. As you work through it, take off every third day to review the workouts that you've already learned. Continue working out in this fashion so that you will not forget the earlier workouts while learning those in the new section. After a while, drop the first few chapters, then later go back and review them before finishing the book. By the time you've reached the end of the book you will be in command of all it contains regarding exercise, movement and nutrition.

The simplest way of adding music to your practice time would probably be to put on the radio, but if you have a favorite disc or tape, then use it. I've suggested some music for a few of the routines and have included this in a Discography near the end of the book, but you may not need it since so much of the music on the radio is excellent for this purpose. Use popular or classical music, or perhaps you'd relish a few moments of silence. Suit yourself.

DANCE, MOVEMENT, AND NUTRITION - Fitness Minutes for a Healthier Life provides you with many aids for learning and remembering the countless movement sequences. You'll find hints on technique for improved performance, suggestions for aerobicizing a movement further, and for simplifying it or taking it to a more advanced level. There are copious photographs to assist you in learning or recalling the movement sequences. The GLOSSARY near the end of the book has definitions and further information that may not be in any other portion of the book. If you wish to see what else the book offers on a particular subject, say lutein, or hamstrings, check the INDEX for page numbers. The Suggested Reading at the end of each chapter and the Bibliography at the end of the book list supplementary reading material for your enjoyment.

Among the NUTRITION HINTS to be found within each chapter are items on food intake versus calorie output that make it easy to understand that good nutritious food together with daily exercise is the secret for maintaining your best weight and for staying fit. You'll find much information on the latest "wonder," the innumerable phytochemicals, powerful antioxidants, to be found in fruits and vegetables of all colors, as well as news about the preferred fats and oils and also the worst ones for you. You'll be reminded that you do not need to know the names of the vitamins, minerals and antioxidants; you simply have to include a variety of different fruits and vegetables, a minimum of fat, salt, and sugar in your meals to be sure that you have a healthy diet. The notes on nutrition are labeled NUTRITION HINTS. There are also three easy recipes that can be varied by changing the ingredients and spices, or adding a little lemon juice, ginger or vinegar. I did not indicate cooking time, which is anywhere from 1/2 an hour to one hour depending on whether you use canned, frozen, fresh, large or small pieces as your ingredients. After all, this is not a cookbook; these recipes are just ideas for foods that are quickly prepared, tasty, and nutritious.

You may find it a good idea to keep a journal of your daily exercises, meals, and water intake. For example: Monday, March 1, a list of all the exercises you did, and all the foods you ate in meals or snacks, and how much water you drank. Make it very detailed or not, as you wish, whatever suits your style and purpose. (Remember to include any walking.) You can write it down consecutively, or in a better format:

Date   Exercises Done   Time Spent   Music   Cooling Down Exercises

Meals: Breakfast –
         Lunch –
         Snack –
         Water –

Try the pinch test before opening the first chapter of **DANCE, MOVEMENT, AND NUTRITION**. Take a pinch of skin at your side under your ribcage. How much flesh do you have between your fingers? Is it 1/4, 1/2, 3/4 of an inch, or more, and how much do you weigh? Now you know how much weight goes with that amount of flesh in a pinch (for you) and you don't have to keep weighing yourself to ascertain approximately what your weight is; 1/2 to 3/4 of an inch means time to watch your calories while one inch or more means start losing pounds now. The 2005 guidelines by the US Department of Agriculture are meant to prevent weight gain and include an eating plan of not more than 2,000 calories a day (to contain at least nine daily servings of fruits and vegetables) and an exercise plan of 30 to 60 minutes of exercise a day, preferably 60 or 90 minutes.

At regular intervals, take the time to evaluate the improvements you have made, say after a month, 3 months, 6 months, or a year; see how much better you feel: trimmer, firmer, better posture, more energetic, more stamina, more flexible, stronger, flatter abdomen, firmer buttocks, or more relaxed, coordinated and confident.

When you've gone through the whole book, one, two or three times, take a moment to ask yourself what you still need. Go through the book and pick out 6 exercises or routines that you feel would be good for your situation. And now when you practice do a whole chapter and just 3 of those extra movements on day one; the next day do the chapter again and the other 3 exercises, so you are not doing all 6 every day. Continue through the book with the addition of those 6 movement sequences. If, after 3 months you wish to change those 6 to a different 6 exercises, do so. You'll be starting to think about your body and   about what it needs, and that is excellent.

DANCE, MOVEMENT, AND NUTRITION - Fitness Minutes for a Healthier Life realizes that many people want the fitness available from doing exercise, and also the alignment, grace and poise associated with dance, such as a good ballroom dancer might have. Another unusual feature to be found in this book is the recommendation to visualize oneself doing a movement accurately, when time and space for its actual execution is out of the question. This book gets away from the prosaic way of presenting workouts; it lets you be the judge of how much time and how many portions of workouts to do at one session or on one day to best suit your needs and life style. The movements and routines in the book are divided into small portions that can easily be absorbed. You choose which sequences need to be repeated more slowly and these will serve for your cooling down section. You are occasionally encouraged to get involved in some of the routines in a creative way, as in ETHNIC FAIR or in the SPORTS OLYMPICS or CREATIVE MIX routines. (However, there is a sufficient amount of direction to suit those who prefer to be told precisely what to do next.) You choose whether to read the Fitness and Nutrition Hints from each Chapter beforehand, as you get to them, or later.

Many people are concerned with staying fit and with helping to prevent heart disease and its leading risk factors: obesity, high blood pressures, high blood cholesterol, and diabetes. Research has shown that your genes may affect your health. While you can't change your genes, there is something positive you can do because the exercise movements you do and the foods you eat are even more important for your health.

DANCE, MOVEMENT, AND NUTRITION - Fitness Minutes for a Healthier Life will help you to stretch, strengthen and relax both the body and mind and give you innumerable hints on pursuing a healthy way of both exercising and eating.

CHAPTER 1 - SPORTS OLYMPICS

No. 1-1 – Torso Stretch to Side

No. 1-2 – Knee to Chest

No. 1-3 – Turnout and Relax

No. 1-4 – Side Extension

No. 1-5 – Hand Flick

Dance Routine – Sports Olympics

Suggested Reading

No. 1-1 – TORSO STRETCH TO SIDE

Stand with the feet parallel, slightly apart and directly under the hips. Hands are clasped in back of the head.

1-2   Bend the knees; at the same time press the elbows back, the hands against the back of the head and the head against the hands. The top of the head reaches up toward the ceiling. Knees should remain lined up over the feet.

3-4   Straighten the legs and extend the arms up straight, with the palms facing up and the fingers still clasped.

5-6   Repeat counts 1-2.

7-8   Straighten the legs and extend the arms high overhead to the right as you tilt the upper torso to the right.

9-12   Repeat counts 1-4.

13-16   Reverse counts 5-8; the torso now tilts to the left.

17-32   Repeat counts 1-16.

33-40   Relax.

41-120   Repeat 2 times, counts 1-40.

When you know this exercise well, try it with stride jumps. Jump with the feet apart as the arms straighten either up or to the right or to the left; then jump with the feet together as the arms return to their position at the back of the head.

Or do the movement without jumps, but with the whole torso bent forward, parallel to the floor. Then bend the knees, with the hands on the head; straighten the knees as the torso and arms reach out and down toward the feet; with the torso relaxed, do heel pulses to make sure that the weight is forward over the balls of the feet.

FITNESS MINUTES: For mild injuries, should they occur, always think of RICE for Rest, Ice (or cold compresses), Compression (but not too tight), and Elevation (to keep swelling to a minimum). And as soon as you feel better, if it is a very mild injury, the E becomes Exercise; stop the Elevation and do some easy relaxed movement but not the one that caused the injury. Be sure to check with your doctor before starting on an exercise program.

NUTRITION HINT: When you eat out very often you need to be aware of portion sizes. If the serving is large, you enjoy the food and hate to see it go to waste, ask for a doggy bag, then put the food in the refrigerator and have it for lunch the next day. It is a well-known fact that portions and plates in restaurants have gradually been getting larger, and that people, too, have likewise been getting larger.

****

No. 1-2 – KNEE TO CHEST

Start on your back in hook lying position. Extend the arms out at the sides with palms up, if space permits; otherwise place the hands under the head with the elbows on the floor.

1-2   Lift the right knee up to the chest while pressing the hips, shoulders and elbows down on the floor. Pull up the abdomen and press your back and belly button down toward the floor.

3-4   Lower the right foot to the floor, next to the left foot, with the knees bent.

5-8   Reverse counts 1-4.

9-32   Repeat 3 times, counts 1-8.

33-40   Relax.

41-80   Repeat counts 1-40.

This movement is an excellent stretch for the lower back and for the hamstrings.

Be sure to relax or press the buttocks down into the floor; they should not lift up as the knee comes toward your chest. Pull in the abdomen as the foot returns to the floor. Do not let the back arch. Press it into the floor.

FITNESS MINUTES: Wear suitable clothing for exercising, something appropriate for the location and temperature. Wear comfortable garments, and stay away from those made of nonporous materials; they hold the moisture in next to your skin and are neither comfortable nor healthy for you. Wear footgear or no shoes, as is suitable, such as barefoot at home and rubber soles on cement. For healthy summer fun, the Medical Society of the State of New York recommends avoiding outdoor exercise between 10 am and 4 pm when the sun's rays are strongest. According to the "Shadow Rule," if your shadow is smaller than you, the sun's damaging ultra violet rays are at their strongest; sunscreen, sunglasses and wide-brimmed hats should be worn outdoors. In the winter, wear layered insulated clothing that will not retain moisture (polyfleece or polypropylene). Wear a windproof outer layer. Keep clothes dry. Wet clothes do not keep their insulating effect and, in combination with wind, can give you a chill. A warm hat and also shoes with enough traction to prevent falls are important, too.

NUTRITION HINT: The United States Department of Agriculture did a study of many diets and found that the percentage of carbohydrates and proteins in them differed from one to the other. Although these diets may not be in agreement on this subject, just about everyone, including the World Health Organization, agrees that to lose weight you must take in fewer calories than the energy (calories) you expend, whether these calories are from carrots, a steak or cookies. A few less calories and a bit more movement, e.g., exercise, walking, stair climbing, house cleaning, on a daily basis, will result in a steady and very gradual weight loss. About half of the adults in the U. S. are overweight, and the percentage of those who are seriously overweight or obese – by 100 pounds or more – is increasing steadily. The most preventable cause of death at this time is obesity.

Now if you really want to lose weight what you should do is: eat healthy foods in which you take pleasure; cut down on your portions; eat less salt, less empty sugar and a minimum of fats (completely eliminating the bad fats); try to lose only one to two pounds per week while exercising regularly. When you lose weight gradually, your body gets used to it; in fact, it hardly notices. But when you lose a lot of weight very quickly your body tries to hoard what's left and not lose it; this defeats your purpose. Always remember that a plump person who walks and exercises is healthier than a plump couch potato and is also more likely to lose a few pounds. If by any chance doing exercise makes you ravenously hungry, then exercise a bit less and eat a bit less.

****

No. 1-3 – TURNOUT AND RELAX

Start on your back, supine, with straight legs; hands are under the head, at the sides or overhead in a wide U.

1-4   Gradually bend the knees out toward the sides, turned out. Place the soles of

the feet together and slowly bring the feet up along the floor, as high as possible. Be sure to keep the waistline down on the floor and the abdomen pulled up.

5-8   Reverse counts 1-4, extend the legs along the floor, with the waistline remaining down, the abdomen pulling up, and the soles of the feet remaining together as long as possible. Then remove the turnout; the knees will face directly up with straight legs and flexed feet.

+9-10   Do 2 low leg raises off the floor with the right leg, reaching out from under the leg to the heel of the flexed foot. Toes reach up as far as possible. Hips do not wiggle. Abdomen pulls up.

11-12   Reverse counts 9-10.

13-16   Repeat counts 9-12.

17-64   Repeat 3 times, counts 1-16.

FITNESS MINUTES: Relaxation is very important for flexibility and muscle balance. As you lie on your back in hook lying position, be aware of the arms and shoulders resting on the floor, either overhead in a wide U, or with the hands under your head or at your sides, and the waistline and hips down on the floor. In that position, lift one knee and slowly make circles with it; reverse the direction of the circles; then try it with the other knee. This should make you more aware of how relaxed you can become with a little bit of thought and effort.

Take the time to concentrate as you do this movement very slowly. The ability to unwind and relax is of prime importance for alleviating stress and tension.

NUTRITION HINT: Anyone planning to follow a specific diet – and there are numerous ones around – should do their homework and check up on the differences between diets, what they include, and what they exclude in the way of foods. Will you be missing valuable nutrients that you could have if you ate a variety of grains, fruits, vegetables and protein? Or will you be eating too much of a particular item, such as saturated fats, which could harm you and is known to be bad for the heart? Can you follow that diet but modify it and eat less of a certain item (such as fats), or include some of what it lacks (be it proteins, carbohydrates or calcium?) Will you lose weight and enhance your health or will you have poorer health in the long run? For good health, many experts who have nothing to gain or to lose from your following their advice advocate a well balanced food plan which includes a variety of fruits, vegetables, grains, low fat dairy, low fat meat and fish, together with a low salt intake and no empty sugar calories.

****

No. 1-4 – SIDE EXTENSION

Start in hook lying position, on your left side. The left hand is under your head; the right one is on the floor in front of you, for support.

1-2   Turn out the top right knee.

3-4   Lift the right knee up toward your shoulder, pressing the opposite hip down on the floor. Try to relax under the thighs.

5-6   Extend the right leg, turned out, to the side or somewhere between the front and true side, with the toes fully pointed.

7-8   Flex the foot of the straight right leg, reaching out under the right leg to the heel.

9-12	Slowly lower the straight right leg.
13-16	Bend the knees and relax.
17-64	Repeat 3 times, counts 1-16.
65-72	Relax on your back. Place your right side on the floor; prepare to reverse the movement with the left leg.
73-136	Reverse counts 1-64.

As you point and flex your foot during this exercise, consider the following: People with feet that arch at the tip, as though the toes were curling under, need to relax the toes and concentrate on stretching the top of the feet near the ankle, to develop this area more fully. Those with a good stretch near the ankle need to concentrate on pointing the toes. If your calves or feet cramp when you try to point or flex them more than usual, shake them out and relax them but don't point or flex them for a few hours.

FITNESS MINUTES: Before starting your exercises, check out your surroundings. Make sure you have sufficient space for possible leg, arm, or torso swings. If the routine demands some traveling movements, is there space for large steps or just small ones? If you intend to hold on to a piece of furniture, is it a good solid piece, unlikely to topple over? And the floor, are any scatter rugs in your way? If you are in the park, how even is the earth? And at the beach, is the sand smooth or full of shells? Once you've checked all this out, you can do your exercises and have fun with the routines. You're prepared.

NUTRITION HINT: If you are trying to maintain your present weight or lose some, it's important to keep portion sizes in mind. For example, 1/2 a bagel is a serving, so is one slice of bread, 3/4 cup of fruit juice, one medium orange, one egg, or 1/2 cup of oatmeal or wheat cereal, 1/2 cup of fat free cottage cheese, 2 tablespoons of peanut butter, one cup of low fat milk or yogurt. It is always a good idea to start the day with breakfast to give you energy for the next few hours of activity; you'll easily use up all the calories you ate if you consumed a reasonable breakfast (and not everything listed in this paragraph.)

****

No. 1-5 – HAND FLICK

Stand with arms at the sides, elbows bent toward the back and the hands in loose fists, wrists close to the hips and palms facing up.

| + | Both arms extend out toward the front left corner; as they do so, the palms face each other and the hands are up higher than the elbows; the elbows are not yet completely straight. |

| 1 | The elbows straighten as the arm extension is completed and the forearms seem to throw the hands out toward the left, with the palms facing down, long fingers hanging toward the floor from the wrists. The torso will tend to pull out toward the opposite right side and lean toward the throwing side – to the left. |

| 2 | Hold the position for a second, then return wrists to the sides of the hips. |

| +3-4 | Reverse counts +1-2 as the arms extend out toward the front right corner. |

| +5-16 | Repeat 3 times, counts +1-4. |

| 17-24 | Relax. |

| 25-96 | Repeat 3 times, counts 1-24. |

For a little more difficulty try this: As you throw the arms and hands out toward downstage left, the front left corner, do small, light jumps toward the right. Then do 2 jumps in place with the feet together as the arms return to the starting position, or do a stride jump – a jump that lands with the feet apart, and then the feet are closed together with another jump.

FITNESS MINUTES: Several years ago the Sports Medicine Committee of the United States Olympic Committee made some excellent comments that still hold true today: Enjoyment is important in order for someone to stick to a particular activity. For a good performance, a well balanced diet is the best. Adequate rest is necessary, especially for those who participate in strenuous physical activity on a daily basis. The consensus was that discipline of mind as well as of body is the ideal. Each person needs to give some thought to his/her physical activities and not just perform them.

NUTRITION HINT: For maximum energy, make it a rule not to skip meals. Plan your day so you have time for meals and snacks to refuel your motor. A healthy diet, with adequate water, is best.

****

DANCE ROUTINE – SPORTS OLYMPICS

Put on your favorite music – one with a bouncy rhythm suitable for doing small running prances and suitable for the Sports Olympics Routine.

| 1-8 | Run in place, lifting the feet up in front. |

9-16   Run in place, lifting the feet up in back.

17-32   Imagine one of your favorite sports: bowling, tennis, skiing, horseback riding, swimming, archery, basketball, etc. Use the arms as you would in one of these sports while running in place.

33-64   Repeat counts 1-16 and use arm movements from a different sport. Make an attempt to vary the type of arm movements, e.g., backstroke or breaststroke arms, dribbling and throwing the basketball up high or turning a jump rope.

65-   Continue in the above fashion until the end of the music. Keep repeating counts 1-16, varying the sport so that you expand the types of movements. When you are feeling comfortable with this activity, try adding torso movements as well. If space allows, travel in some sort of floor pattern, such as forward and backward, a circle, figure 8, or a letter of the alphabet – whatever suits you.

Start slowly as you do this sequence, then gradually lift the knees up higher and use larger movements. Take about four minutes to do the Dance Routine. Slow down then accelerate again; just be sure to keep the movement continuous. You may even start by walking instead of running in place. If you are listening to the radio you might like to change the rhythm of your movement to go with the music being played on the radio. The main concern is to keep it non-stop, have fun, and do an assortment of arm movements as you repeat this series of exercises and routine for the next two weeks or so.

FITNESS MINUTES: For a cooling-down movement, practice anything you feel you need, provided you do it slowly. If you have been practicing vigorously, do something simple, e.g., No. 1-1, Torso Stretch to Side. If you are tired and would love to lie down for a bit before the end of your workout, here's your chance – practice some of the earlier warm-ups which you did while lying down on the floor, e.g., No. 1-2, Knee to Chest, but more slowly, and concentrate on your breathing – very relaxed and full – from the abdomen. If you feel especially energetic, then do a previous exercise slowly for the maximum stretch and best technique, e.g., No. 1-4. For cooling-down, sit, lie down or stand; suit yourself.

NUTRITION HINT: Always check the labels and list of ingredients on food items. Avoid those with trans fats or partially hydrogenated fats. These bad fats are found in some packaged foods such as cereals, cookies, frozen meals, stick margarine and fried fast foods. They promote heart damage by raising the level of LDL (bad cholesterol), while lowering HDL (good cholesterol). Eating foods with soluble fiber, such as apples, citrus fruits, beans, grains, soybeans and especially oats and oatmeal, is one way of fighting back; it helps the liver dispose of surplus LDL. Soy beans are a bit salty, but added to a green leafy salad, they're delicious, as is tofu, which is also made of soy. (Remember to check the Glossary and Index for further information.)

****

SUGGESTED READING

"America's Obesity Crisis." *Time Magazine,* June 7, 2004, Pgs. 57-113.

Cheney, Gay. *Basic Concepts in Modern Dance, A Creative Approach*, 3rd Edition. Pennington, NJ: A Dance Horizons Book, Princeton Book Company, Publishers, 1989.

Lindsay, Ruth, Billie J. Jones and Ada Van Whitley. *Body Mechanics.* William C Brown and Co., 1974.

Webb, Geoffrey P. BSc, MSc, PhD. *Nutrition, A Health Promotion Approach.* London: Arnold, A member of the Hodder Headline Group, 1995.

CHAPTER 2 - ETHNIC FAIR

No. 2-1 – TWIST AND SWING

Stand with the feet slightly apart and parallel; arms are down at the sides.

1-2   Twist the upper torso to the right, while swinging the arms down and up toward the right in an easy and relaxed manner. Be sure that the hips remain facing directly forward.

3-4   Reverse – twist the torso to the left and swing the arms down toward the left.

5-16   Repeat 3 times, counts 1-4.

17-18 Bend the knees – plié.

19-20 Straighten the legs.

21-22   Rise on the balls of the feet – relevé.

23-24   Lower the heels with straight legs.

25-32   Repeat counts 17-24.

33-34   Bend the knees and contract the hips by tightening the buttocks and tucking under and toward the front.

35-36   Hips are centered with knees bent.

37-38   Release the hips – relax the buttocks and press them back and up.

39-40   Hips are centered with knees bent.

41-160   Repeat 3 times, counts 1-40.

On counts 1-16 look down at your right hip and make sure that it does not move as you twist the upper torso to the right. Keep the torso twist movement small at first. Your hip should stay in place so you can see it; otherwise you'll feel like a puppy chasing its tail and never catching up with it.

For a more aerobic movement, once you know the movement well, add small, light jumps on both feet or three running jumps in place as you twist the upper torso to that side; then reverse.

The beginning and middle sections of this exercise, the torso twist and plié and relevé, could be used as a cooling-down movement at the end of your workout.

FITNESS MINUTES: As you go through this book remember to do it at your pace. When you have gone through the book once and find yourself going faster as you go through it a second or third time, with more repetitions of each sequence or more repetitions of the whole sequence of exercises before doing the routine many times, you may find your muscles getting tired, sore or tight. If this happens, take off one day a week, or a few days, if you really need it, till your body feels restored.

NUTRITION HINT: To prevent dehydration when exercising take care to drink a sufficient amount of liquids – water, unsweetened fruit juice or broth, but not coffee or alcohol – to replenish the body's water supply. This is especially true in the summer. However, there may be no need for you to drink 8 glasses of water daily if you get sufficiently hydrated from the amount of other beverages that you drink, as well as from fruits and vegetables. Beverages that contain caffeine – coke, tea or coffee – are not included because they are diuretics and cause the body to lose water. For the kidneys to function properly it is important to drink a sufficient amount of water in order to dilute all the wastes that the body excretes and to help prevent kidney stones.

Dehydration can also cause fatigue, chronic constipation, shriveled skin, and muscle cramps by decreasing blood circulation, thus limiting the amount of oxygenated blood received by the muscles. When cells in the body are dehydrated, they draw water from the blood, which then becomes thick. Your body needs to exert more energy to pump the blood, and fatigue sets in. People who live in excessively hot climates or who do arduous or prolonged physical activity may need the 8 glasses or more of water, besides the fruits and vegetables, likewise those who follow a weight loss regime advising a glass of water before and during each meal.

A study by the International Journal of Sport Nutrition found that contrary to what people used to say, one to four cups of coffee per day does not lead to dehydration in people doing exercise, provided they drink water.

Since an excess of water can also be bad for you (especially for the long distance marathon runners drinking extreme amounts of water), thirst is a good indication that water should be drunk. The color of your urine is likewise indicative of your water intake; pale is fine but dark means you need to drink more water; there is a high concentration of body waste in the urine. One or two glasses of water before breakfast is excellent for getting rid of body waste and preventing constipation.

****

No. 2-2 – LONG LEG SITTING - PULSES

Start by sitting on the floor with the legs straight and close together. The feet are flexed and the heels reach forward as much as possible. The arms should be forward, with slightly bent elbows and with the hands in jazz hand position – hands stretched wide with the fingers far apart.

1	Shoulders go forward with the arms in starting position – jazz hands and slightly bent elbows.
2	Shoulders move back.
3-8	Repeat 3 times, counts 1-2.

9-16	With the torso do 4 small pulses forward from the hips, with the torso straight, the shoulders back and the feet flexed.
17-24	Now repeat counts 1-8, with shoulder movement forward and back, and with the feet pointing and the ankles fully stretched.
25-32	Repeat counts 9-16, 4 small, bouncy pulses forward from the hips, but now with the feet pointing.
33-40	Relax the rounded torso, with the arms and hands forward over the legs; then straighten the torso up tall, with the arms circling overhead through the front, then out to the sides and forward. At this point the elbows bend and the hands are once more stretched wide in jazz hand position.
41-160	Repeat 3 times, counts 1-40.

FITNESS MINUTES: Pulsing movements, or ballistic movements as they are called, are often used in exercises and in dance warm-ups. They have been found not to be as effective as just relaxing while holding a position for 20-30 seconds. However, both are good – the passive stretch and the ballistic stretch. There are times when you might prefer a slow, easy pulsing ballistic movement, such as in extremely hot, humid weather, or if you tend to overstretch and pull muscles easily

when you do a relaxed passive stretch. Also, you might use it for variety, because it's an interesting movement, very basic to jazz music, dance and body rhythms – pulse beat equals heart beat. Just make it a gentle pulse.

NUTRITION HINT: When trying to change your figure or weight don't compare yourself to others, but consider yourself and your goals and aim for that challenge. After sticking to your exercise schedule and your efforts at better nutrition for two weeks, or after finishing one chapter of this book, give yourself a small reward – say a new skin moisturizer or a cooking spice. (A can of low-salt chicken broth with the addition of a variety of spices and garlic or onion powder makes a satisfying warm broth with very few calories but lots of healthy antioxidants from the spices; and in the summer it's a cool refreshing drink from the fridge.) Check the Glossary for health benefits obtained from various spices: thyme, tarragon, garlic, turmeric, ginger, basil, etc.

****

No. 2-3 – TURNOUT ROLLS

Sit on the floor with the soles of the feet together, the legs turned out and the hands on the floor in back of you.

1-2	Relax the left knee out to the left side as much as possible, while rolling over toward the right side till the right knee is on the floor.
3-4	Reverse counts 1-2.
5-16	Repeat 3 times, counts 1-4.
17-24	Stretch the legs straight out in front and bend them in again as you circle the arms up overhead, to the sides, and return the hands to the floor as before.

25-96   Repeat 3 times, counts 1-24.

This exercise should be done with a relaxed, comfortable feeling, no strain. It is relaxing for the legs following the previous exercise in long-leg sitting position.

FITNESS MINUTES: Throughout the book there are reminders of the many benefits to be obtained from a dance, exercise and fitness workout such as this one. They have been purposely placed here and there, rather than all in one chapter, so that you will be constantly reminded of the many assets of your workout, and you will make these fitness minutes of exercise and healthy eating a habit and a way of having a happy, sound and fulfilling life.

NUTRITION HINT: The Pregnancy & Newborn Health Education Center at the March of Dimes recommends three to four servings of proteins per day for a healthy diet for pregnant and nursing women. Protein is responsible for strong blood and muscles. The Center advises them to eat low fat meat and a limited amount of processed meats. Protein sources include: chicken, turkey, pork, lamb, beef, fish, shellfish, eggs, canned baked beans, peas/beans, tofu, peanut butter and nuts.

****

No. 2-4 – CURL AND ARCH

Start by lying supine – on your back – with the arms extended out at the sides on the floor, with the palms up. The legs are straight, slightly apart and parallel.

1-6   As the upper torso, the head, knees and the feet curl up off the floor in a semicircular fashion, the arms swing down to your sides on the floor and then come forward to hold the feet at the sides, or if that is not possible, then they hold the legs from under the knees. The waistline remains flat on the floor. The

knees are up toward the raised head. The abdomen is pulled up with the belly button pressing the waistline down toward the floor as you hold that position. Continue breathing normally; do not hold your breath.

20

| 7-8 | Stretch out flat, with straight legs on the floor. At the same time the arms go down at the sides and then swing up along the floor at the sides. |

| 9-14 | The arms continue the movement and go overhead through the sides as you roll over on your right side, with the whole body arching toward the back. The two arms, overhead, round toward the back with the hands farther back than the elbows. The hips are pressed forward; the knees are together and slightly bent so the legs can continue the long arching bodyline. |

| 15-16 | Roll over to your back with a flat back and straight legs as you swing the arms from their position overhead to the sides along the floor. |

| 17-32 | Reverse counts 1-16. |

| 33-128 | Repeat 3 times, counts 1-32. |

Do this exercise slowly at first to get the full benefit of the stretching, but when you know it well do it several times at a snappier pace, or follow it up with one or two other exercises, and do them for two to ten minutes without stopping and without getting out of breath.

This is an excellent exercise for the abdomen and it also provides a stretch for the antagonistic muscles – opposing muscle group of the torso and legs – as you move from the curled up to the arched body position.

FITNESS MINUTES: Should you find that an exercise causes you pain as you do it, stop. There are many exercises for each area of the body. Try a different exercise until you are in better condition – especially if you are working out by yourself. As you go through the book you'll find other exercises that you'll prefer for that area of the body. If you are taking a class, ask your instructor for a solution to your problems.

NUTRITION HINT: An excellent way to be sure to have some of all the antioxidants that we need for good health is to eat a very varied and colorful meal. The rich and darker colors are those containing the most of a particular antioxidant: dark green leafy vegetables, such as spinach, kale, broccoli, or bok choy (full of vitamins A and C, fiber, folate, indoles, cancer blocking chemicals, and lutein); dark red: tomatoes, watermelon, red and pink grapefruit (lycopene fights heart disease, prevents UV – ultraviolet – damage); yellow/green: corn, green peas, honeydew or squash (lutein and zeaxanthin for reduced risk of macular degeneration and cataracts); orange: carrots, cantaloupes, pumpkin, apricots, yams (alpha-carotene and beta-carotene are cancer fighting antioxidants); rich dark red/purple: blueberries, blackberries, plums, prunes, purple cabbage, eggplants, beets (the antioxidant betaine detoxifies excess amino acids, and anthocyanin inhibits blood clot formation and improves vision); light colored white/green: celery, leek, garlic, asparagus, green grapes, and onions (the onion family has allicin and quercetin that protect the heart and lungs, and all of these have antioxidant flavonoids and cholesterol-lowering antioxidants, especially garlic).

Regardless of the name of all these antioxidants, or which food has what, a meal with a diversity of colors will offer you a wide range of antioxidants and nutrients. Besides being an attractive meal it will be a healthy one. Always include at least nine servings of an assortment of fruits and vegetables in your daily diet. If one of these antioxidants should be isolated in a supplement, it will not be as beneficial as the food itself where it operates in conjunction with the numerous other nutrients to be found in each food source. Phytonutrients are only obtained from plant sources, not from animal products. Fliers from some supermarkets even include reminders to shop for a variety of colors when eating out or buying produce.

****

No. 2-5 – LEG RAISE, FRONT TO SIDE

Start on your back with feet slightly apart, parallel, and flexed. The legs are straight. Arms are either extended out at the sides with the palms facing up, or under your head with the elbows down on the floor.

1+ Lift the right leg up to the front, about 2 to 3 inches. The feet are flexed

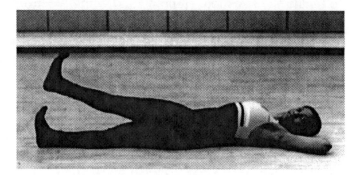

throughout. The abdomen remains pulled up, both of the shoulders are down, and the hips are motionless with no side-to-side rocking movement.

2 Lower the right leg.

3-4 Repeat counts 1-2, again with the right leg.

22

5-8	Reverse counts 1-4 and do 2 low leg raises with the left leg.
9-12	Do 1 slow, high leg raise in front – as high as comfortable – with the right leg, taking 2 counts to raise and 2 counts to lower the leg.
13-16	Reverse counts 9-12.
17-18	Raise right leg high in front.
19-20	Carry the straight right leg to the side as far as possible, keeping the shoulders and the other leg immobile.
21-22	From the side, carry the right leg up in front.
23-24	Lower the right leg, being sure to pull up the abdomen.
25-32	Reverse counts 17-24.
33-128	Repeat 3 times, counts 1-32.

One of the nice things about a lying-down warm up is that it gives you a change from your usual standing or sitting position. This is an excellent idea for people who sit or stand constantly at work.

FITNESS MINUTES: Remember to check the Glossary and the Index for any further information to be found in this book on a particular subject or word.

NUTRITION HINT: Antioxidants, so numerous in fruits and vegetables, are of benefit to us because they fight free radicals – toxic materials that are byproducts of the oxidative processes in cells and that are produced by the body during our daily activities: digesting and breathing various compounds such as medications, rancid fats, hydrogenated oils, inhaled components of air pollution, and other damaging sources. Free radicals are actually unattached oxygen molecules, lacking one electron. If they bind with healthy cells, these then become unbalanced and a destructive chain reaction is in progress, leading to the creation of more free radicals.

These free radicals, which can cause harm to organs and lead to cancer, impaired immune functions and heart disease, are resisted by the body's elaborate antioxidant system. This natural resistance by the body often needs to be supplemented by antioxidants in the diet to ensure minimum harm by free radicals; for example, beta-carotene and vitamins C and E have strong antioxidant properties; they function as free radical scavengers and have the ability to oppose and quench free radicals.

****

DANCE ROUTINE – ETHNIC FAIR

Put on the radio. Look for music with an ethnic flavor, or your favorite station of classical or popular music. Make do with whatever is playing; every time you practice you'll have a different rhythm for inspiration; you'll never get bored.

1-8	Run in place, lifting the feet up in front.
9-16	Run in place, lifting the feet up in back.
17-32	You've heard of Ethnic Food Fairs; well this is an Ethnic Movement Fair. Think of a variety of arm, head, and torso movements used by ethnic dance groups. They can be either stereotyped or very authentic ones. Here are a few suggestions: the Hawaiian Hula's wavelike arm movements to the sides; East Indian's head movements from right to left; Sicilian tarantella's finger snapping overhead; Spanish Flamenco dancer's rounded arms to the front and back; Caribbean shoulders alternately going forward and back; even an American Charleston with the palms out in front would be fun. Find more yourself, from Russia, Africa, the Far East, etc.
33-	Continue till the end of the music. Repeat the running in place of counts 1-16, and then add another ethnic dance type of arm and torso movement. Continue in this manner till the end of 3-4 minutes of non-stop movement. Walk instead of running whenever you wish. Then return to the running either in place or traveling, as the space permits.

FITNESS MINUTES: Even in the 18th Century, aerobics was promoted for fitness, as was shown on a PBS program about travels in England with "Rick Steve's Europe." The fitness seeker sat on a Chippendale exercising chair having horizontal extensions overhead; the hands held onto these extensions. The bottom of the chair included some sort of spring which caused the person who was sitting on the seat of the chair to bounce up and down on the seat as the feet moved on the base of the chair as though doing light jumps. It must have felt somewhat like riding on a bouncy horse; only it was an indoor activity.

NUTRITION HINT: Breakfast is considered by many to be the most important meal of the day; it energizes you right at the start of the day. It should include a small amount of each of the following: carbohydrates – whole grains and fruit – which will get broken down into glucose to give you quick energy and will supply phytochemicals (also called phytonutrients or micronutrients) from plant sources to reduce the risk of heart disease and help prevent cancer. Vitamin C, from citrus fruits or berries, is needed to maintain the immune system, to help digest iron from plant sources, to help digest fiber to keep your blood-sugar level stable, to do away with drops in energy and to minimize food cravings. Vitamin B from whole grains will keep your nervous and digestive systems functioning properly.

Breakfast should also include some protein – an egg, yogurt, low fat milk, low fat cheese, or low fat meat – whose amino acids are needed to maintain muscle tissue and keep them repaired. The calcium (from dairy) in your breakfast – low fat milk or low fat cheese – will help your body burn fat instead of holding onto it. Fats, such as those from low fat dairy foods – monounsaturated fats – are also necessary and will help in the absorption of fat-soluble vitamins A, D, E, and K and keep your nervous system healthy. One half a teaspoon of cinnamon on your cereals daily can help maintain the blood sugar level and lower bad cholesterol and triglycerides.

****

SUGGESTED READING

Heber, David, Dr. with Susan Bowerman. *What Color Is Your Diet?* New York, N.Y.: Regan Books, an imprint of HarperCollins Publishers, Inc., 2001.

Jones, Jeanne. *Canyon Ranch Cooking: Bringing the Spa Home.* NY, NY: HarperCollins Publishers, Inc., 1998.

Nagrin, Daniel. *How to Dance Forever: Surviving Against the Odds.* NY: William Morrow, 1988.

"Your Health – What's Worse Than Sugar?" *AARP Bulletin,* April 2004.

CHAPTER 3 - PLAYFUL SAMBA

No. 3-1 – Hip Contraction

No. 3-2 – Front Extension

No. 3-3 – Leg and Torso Toner

No. 3-4 – Shoulder Rolls

No. 3-5 – Samba Arms

Dance Routine – Playful Samba

Suggested Reading

No. 3-1 – HIP CONTRACTION

Start with the feet slightly apart and parallel; knees are bent; elbows are out to the sides with the hands in flat palm position and fingertips on hipbones at the sides.

1   Release the hips. (See No. 2-1, counts 37-38.)

2   Contract the hips. (See No. 2-1, counts 35-36.)

3-8   Repeat 3 times, counts 1-2.

9+10 Repeat the movement and do it in threes – release, contract, release and pause.

11+12 Contract, release, contract and pause.

13-16 Repeat counts 9-12.

17-64 Repeat 3 times, counts 1-16.

How about doing two small jumps in place for each contraction and release of the hips on counts 1-8; or, if you prefer, do a small sliding movement forward on two feet – a chug – as you contract and then a chug to the back as you release the hips.

FITNESS MINUTES: If you are on the heavy side and hope to lose some weight as you proceed with these movements, try to work out at first, perhaps, for short intervals every day or several times a week. You will notice that your stamina, coordination, flexibility, strength, endurance and confidence will gradually increase. At that point you may want to add some cross training to your fitness activities with a longer workout through participation in a class in your vicinity. An enjoyable one might be Pilates, ballet, ice skating, kick boxing, yoga, belly dancing, or maybe the ever-popular tango, samba or tap dancing. As for the weight, it will come off gradually and that's the best way; it's less traumatic for the body and more likely to stay off. Read the many hints on nutrition that are scattered throughout the book.

NUTRITION HINT: Nutrition experts from the Harvard School of Public Health have created what they believe is a Healthy Eating Pyramid based on the latest scientific links between diet and health. The pyramid can be found at their website http://www.hsph.harvard.edu/nutritionsource/pyramids.html. The pyramid sits on a foundation of daily exercise and weight control, exactly what this book is trying to suggest. The next large block on the triangle is cut in half vertically with whole grain foods, to be eaten at most meals, on one side, and plant oils, like canola, soy, olive, peanut, corn, and vegetable oils, on the other side, because the body does need some fat. These are the healthy fats that can protect the heart. The block above that one is also divided vertically, with vegetables in abundance on one side and 2-3 fruits on the other side. The next block is nuts and legumes 1-3 times a day. Above that is the layer with fish, poultry, and eggs, to be eaten 0-2 times a day, with a note that an egg is far better for you than a bagel from refined flour or a doughnut cooked in an oil that is rich in trans fats. Above this is the block with no fat or low fat dairy, or calcium supplements 1-2 times a day (if you don't care for dairy).

We are now at the top of the pyramid, and it is divided vertically with red meat and butter (use sparingly) on one side; both have lots of saturated fats. The other half of that top block has white rice, white bread, potatoes (without the skin), pasta and sweets (to be used sparingly). These are the items that can cause rapid increases in blood sugar and lead to obesity, diabetes, heart disease and other chronic illnesses. (Whole grain carbohydrates, on the other hand, have none of these injurious effects.) These experts also recommend a multiple vitamin/mineral supplement – a standard store brand that meets the requirements of the USP (U.S. Pharmacopeia) is fine – and one small glass of wine per day, since numerous studies have found that a moderate amount of red wine a day lowers the risk of heart disease.

****

No. 3-2 – FRONT EXTENSION

Start in hook lying position – both knees bent.

1-2   Lift the bent right knee up toward the chest; hips remain down on the floor.

3-4   Extend the right leg and point the toes; the knee is straight.

5-6   Flex the foot of the right leg and try to lift the straight leg higher, with the hips remaining even and on the floor. Abdomen pulls up.

7-10	Slowly lower the right leg, relax the shoulders, and pull in the abdomen.
11-12	Bend the right knee to hook lying position.
13-24	Reverse counts 1-12.
25-96	Repeat 3 times, counts 1-24.

FITNESS MINUTES: One method of making sure that you are not holding your breath while exercising by yourself is to talk. You have a chance to try this out while doing this exercise. Every time you pull up your abdomen on counts 5-6, and on counts 7-10 and after, say "flat, flat tummy," or "abdomen in," or something similar. Then you have the hands tapping the flat tummy to make sure that it is flat, and the words reminding you to flatten the abdomen more; and you're not holding your breath. If you find that this system works well, make up your own catchy phrases for other movements; a phrase that serves as a reminder for better performance can be an asset. Another method of not holding your breath, if you tend to do so while exercising, is to inhale slowly for two full counts, and then exhale for the next two full counts; don't inhale quickly, then hold your breath. Take the full two counts for each inhalation.

NUTRITION HINT: Get in the habit of checking food labels so as to cut down or eliminate from your purchases those items that contain hydrogenated or trans fats. Hydrogenation is a process used to add hydrogen atoms to unsaturated fats to make them more saturated, as in margarine and shortenings, as well as in cakes, cookies and other snack foods. By January 1, 2006, the FDA will require use of trans fats to be listed on food labels.

****

No. 3-3 – LEG AND TORSO TONER

Start in a prone position (on your abdomen) with straight legs; hands are under the chin.

+	Raise the right leg low in back – maybe two inches. The foot is flexed and the hips are on the floor; the leg is straight and presses out to the flexed foot.
1	Place the ball of the flexed right foot – straight leg – on the floor.
+	Lift the straight right leg off the floor and point the toes of the right foot.
2	Place the leg on the floor with the toes pointed.
+3-4	Reverse counts +1+2. This is a good exercise for toning up the buttocks.
5-16	Repeat 3 times, counts 1-4. Be sure to press the heels out and feel the leg lengthening and straightening completely.

17-20	Place the hands on the floor under the shoulders and raise the upper torso.

21-24	Lower the upper torso and relax.

25-32	Repeat counts 17-24. Do not hold your breath or clamp your teeth.

33-48	Place your hands on your back, near your waistline, and raise and lower the upper torso 2 times, taking 4 counts to raise and 4 counts to lower the upper torso.

49-64	Place the hands on the floor under the shoulders. Lift the hips up; sit back on your heels, with your head on your knees; arms are either in front or in back at your sides, whichever is more comfortable.

65-68	Place the right foot on the floor in front. Kneel up and then stand up tall.

69-72	Place the right foot on the floor in back, kneel and return to starting position.

73-144	Reverse counts 1-72.

145-148	Repeat counts 65 to 68.

To be sure not to clamp your teeth together, place the tip of your tongue against the upper gum ridge. Lift the corners of the mouth to promote a pleasant look.

FITNESS MINUTES: No time to practice every day. How about a little exercise for the mind? Keeping the mind alert and interested has been found to be excellent, especially for the elderly. Sometimes just thinking about the steps, dance routines, warm-ups or Fitness Minutes while sitting in the bus or subway can help both the mind and the body. Think about pulling in your abdomen, lengthening the spine, eating healthy foods, being aware of a well-centered body, and relaxing. If you are taking a class, jotting down a few notes for yourself after the class – at home, or on the bus – will help to make you more mindful of some of the pointers you want to remember from the class. You can always look at these the next day at a work break, at lunch, or on the train, when you do not have the time to practice. Visualize yourself doing them, and think through what you need to concentrate on in order to achieve your goals. You won't feel so rusty when you do get to practice or take a class, because your mind will have been thinking along correct lines in preparation for the next workout.

NUTRITION HINT: Studies have found that a combination of changes in lifestyle achieve the best results for those trying to lower their blood pressure. Omitting salt from the diet (one rich in fruits, vegetables, grains, low fat dairy products, and with very little meat), getting an aerobic workout such as a brisk walk per day, losing a few pounds and practicing relaxation techniques, such as slow deep breathing a few times a day, or yoga or meditation are ideal.

****

No. 3-4 – SHOULDER ROLLS

Start with the feet slightly apart and parallel. Face downstage right – the front right corner. Before doing the movements with the counts as written here, try the following with both arms down at the sides: Bring both shoulders way up to your ears and down – 8 times. Then bring the two shoulders forward and back 8 times. Now circle both shoulders 4 times forward, up, back and down. You are ready to proceed.

1	Step to the side toward upstage left – the left back corner – with the left foot. At the same time place the arms to the sides with the palms facing down.
2-3	Pull the right foot in toward the left foot with the ball of the right foot on the floor and the right knee bending, as the right foot comes in next to the left one. At that point start to circle the right shoulder forward to do 2 shoulder rolls – up, to the back and down.
4	Continue the 2nd shoulder circle and place the heel of the right foot down on the floor.
5-12	Repeat 2 times, counts 1-4.

13-16   Relax the arms and face downstage right, or the front right corner, and get ready to reverse counts 1-16. Later, when you are used to the movement, omit these 4 counts and change direction during the first step on the reverse side.

17-32   Reverse counts 1-16.

33-128   Repeat 3 times, counts 1-32.

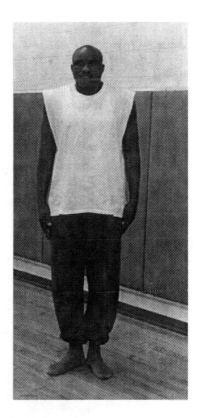

At first, try the shoulder rolls with both shoulders at the same time and with the arms hanging down at the sides.

As you do the shoulder roll, the head looks down at the shoulder while it comes around in a sexy shoulder roll.

If you wish, do the original movements of counts 1-2 on count 1; pull the right foot in on count 2 instead of on counts 3-4; then on new counts 3-4 do 2 shoulder rolls while doing 2 running jumps in place, and continue in this manner. Or run for 8 counts while doing shoulder rolls with the right shoulder, and reverse.

FITNESS MINUTES: If you are not accustomed to doing exercise, or have not been doing any recently, you need to start slowly. But you may still occasionally get a charley horse – a somewhat sore, stiff muscle – from lack of use of a particular muscle. When this occurs, take a hot bath; do not discontinue the exercise, but instead do a little bit, slowly, every day till the muscle feels better.

NUTRITION HINT: Saturated fats are hard at room temperature and are found in animal sources: red meat, poultry, cheese, whole milk, deli meats, butter, and in tropical oils: coconut, palm kernel, and cocoa butter, as well as products made from hydrogenated oils. They should be a minimal portion of your food allowance, since this fat gets stored near your vital organs and can lead to heart disease and diabetes. Hydrogenation is a process used by manufacturers to transform polyunsaturated fats such as vegetable oils, through the addition of hydrogen atoms, so that these fats will solidify to make shortening and some margarines for use in packaged foods that will then be more shelf stable. The trans fats and partially hydrogenated fats thus created are found in doughnuts, cookies, cakes, crackers, frozen meals, fried fast foods, and some cereals, and they are bad for you. Read the food labels and avoid them. Luckily we are able to purchase low fat milk and cheese, buy low fat cuts of meat, or remove excess fats from some meats and the skin from poultry before cooking them.

****

No. 3-5 – SAMBA ARMS

Start with the feet parallel and slightly apart, and the knees relaxed.

1-2 Place the fingertips of the right hand on the ribcage at the center of the upper torso; at the same time extend the left arm out to the side, with the palm facing down, long extended fingers and a slight break in the wrist. Lean back slightly from the hips, since this torso swaying back and front is so much a part of the Playful Samba routine.

3-4 Reverse and place the fingertips of the left hand on the ribcage and the right hand out to the side while leaning forward from the hips.

5-12 Repeat 2 times, counts 1-4.

13-16 Pause and relax the arms.

17-32 Reverse – now lean back from the hips as the left hand comes in front and lean forward from the hips when the right hand comes in front – fingertips on the ribcage.

33-64 Repeat counts 1-32.

65-128 Repeat counts 1-64 and try to stretch the arms more as you do this.

This is an excellent movement for the arms. Have fun with it and keep the arms relaxed. Try doing some jumps in place, or some light runs in a circle or in a figure 8, or forward and back. Then maybe add a head movement and look out toward the extended arm; or add a step and point or kick the leg in front, with or without a jump but with the back and front torso sway and with the arm movements of the samba.

FITNESS MINUTES: It is important to start slowly in an exercise program. Be sure you know all the exercises, steps, and routines if you intend to energize them in a snappy continuous manner for 20 to 30 minutes. Even 5 to 10 minutes is good if your time is limited.

NUTRITION HINT: Welcome news for lovers of chocolate. It contains antioxidants that are good for you. The dark bittersweet variety has more flavonoids (see Glossary) than milk chocolate and about the same amount as half a cup of tea; flavonoids are the reason why tea and bittersweet chocolate are so good for your heart. The fat in chocolate will not lead to more cholesterol in your blood due to the type of fat it is – stearic acid. By itself the chocolate will not give you cavities; combined with syrupy fillings and caramel, it will. The amount of caffeine in an ounce of milk chocolate is low; in an ounce of dark chocolate or a cup of hot cocoa it is 20 milligrams – half the amount of what is in a cup of tea; coffee has 115 milligrams. The only bad news regarding chocolate is that if you eat too much you'll gain weight; it does contain lots of calories – about 140-150 calories per ounce. So eat a small amount – 1/4 of an ounce; eat it slowly, savor it and cut out some other calories to compensate. A small piece for dessert would be delicious.

****

DANCE ROUTINE – PLAYFUL SAMBA

Put on a good samba or any music with a Latin beat; also suitable is any lively tune, like "Bo Diddley".

1+2   Take 3 steps to the right (step to the side on the right, cross the left foot in front, step to the side on the right foot with the left leg extending diagonally back between side and back, and the left arm extending out to the side.) The right hand is on the hip at the side.

3+4   Do 2 shoulder rolls with the left shoulder – forward, up, back, and in place.

5-8   Reverse counts 1-4.

9-12   Repeat counts 1-4.

13+   Step to the side on the left foot and point the right foot crossed in front of it with the right hand going in front of the ribs and the left hand out at the side.

14+   Reverse counts 13+.

15-16 Repeat counts 13-14+.

17-32 Reverse counts 1-16.

33-64 Repeat counts 1-32, but on counts 13-16 instead of pointing the foot in front, touch the ball of the foot on the floor in back. Both knees are bent. Arms are the same as on counts 1-32.

65-   Repeat from the beginning, but now run through it. Instead of walking do running steps. On counts 3-4 jump onto two feet – one in front and one in back – as you do shoulder rolls. On counts 13-16 do small leaps to the side and either touch the foot on the floor to the front, or to the back, or do a small kick to either direction.

Spend about 3-4 minutes on this routine. You may walk through it, run through it, and continue walking and running through it; then maybe finish with a very slow sexy, seductive walk-through of the routine. You can consider this last walk as your cooling down movement, unless you wish to slowly repeat some previous movement from this chapter.

FITNESS MINUTES: Add more movement to your life in convenient segments: Take a walk at a shopping mall; park farther away from the store than you usually would; carry your groceries (a shopping bag in each arm); go up or down a few flights of stairs; go out to buy the newspaper before breakfast if you don't have to walk a dog, or take a break for lunch and go for a quick walk to mail a letter or birthday card. For a change of pace while using the computer or reading, stand up and stretch the arms up (think high – toward the sky) out to the sides then down toward the floor, or do circular movements with the shoulders, arms, and head; one hour of exercise (physical activity) a day is the recommended amount and all of these movements count as physical activity. An inactive lifestyle may lead to cardiac problems by lessening the heart's ability to pump blood and thus augmenting the risk for hypertension, high cholesterol and high blood pressure.

NUTRITION HINT: Should you find yourself getting a very painful "stitch" (pain) in your side while exercising, it could be that you either ate too much or not enough. Try to eat a little bit of something that always agrees with you – perhaps graham crackers and peanut butter or turkey slices on rye bread – about 1/2 to 3/4 hour before exercising. If you have a stitch in your side, drop your torso, head and arms down toward the floor; relax; let your abdomen stick out; don't pull your tummy in tight, while you take a big slow relaxed breath from your abdomen, several times. When you finish class, drink some warm broth or soup and probably nothing else till the pain has subsided. Warm cream of wheat or split pea soup would certainly be good, too.

****

SUGGESTED READING

Audy, Robert. *Tap Dancing – How to Teach Yourself.* NY: Random House, 1976.

Barry, Suzanne. *Basic Pilates.* NY: Barnes and Noble, Inc., 2004.

Shipley, Glenn. *Modern Tap Dictionary.* Los Angeles: Action Marketing Group, 1976.

"Healthy Eating Pyramid." *Harvard School of Public Health,* http://www.hsph.harvard.edu/ nutritionsource/pyramids.html, 2/19/04.

Shook, Karel. *Elements of Classical Ballet Technique, as practiced in the school of the Dance Theatre of Harlem.* NY: Dance Horizons, 1977.

Stuart, Muriel. *The Classical Ballet: Technique and Terminology.* NY: Knopf, 1962.

CHAPTER 4 - COOKIE JAR JUMP

No. 4-1 – Hook Sitting Sit-ups

No. 4-2 – Low and High Leg Raises

No. 4-3 – Arm Flings

No. 4-4 – Leg Raise – Back

No. 4-5 – Stretch and Yawn

Dance Routine – Cookie Jar Jump

Suggested Reading

No. 4-1 – HOOK SITTING SIT-UPS

Start in hook sitting position – knees bent – and hands under your thighs, holding them.

1-4   Roll down your spine till your waistline gets to the floor. Be sure it is your waistline that is on the floor and not your hips. To facilitate this, tuck the hips under and allow one vertebra after the other to touch the floor. Place a towel, small pillow,  mat, etc., under your bones if they feel sore, so that you can concentrate on performing the exercise more correctly. Be sure to keep the feet flat on the floor; think of them as being heavy. Keep the chin close to your chest and the upper torso rounded. Continue rounding the hips under until the waistline is on the floor. Your belly button keeps pulling up and back toward your spine throughout. If the back of your neck gets sore from this head position, then focus your eyes on the ceiling, so your head won't go too far down.

5-8   Roll up to a straight back, in hook sitting position, with the top of the head reaching up toward the ceiling and the shoulders held back.

9-16   Repeat counts 1-8.

17-20   Repeat counts 1-4. Roll down to your waistline.

21-24   Roll down the rest of the way till your upper torso is flat on the floor and the arms are overhead on the floor with the shoulders relaxed down.

25-28   Extend the legs along the floor, slowly, and flatten the waistline down toward the floor.

29-32   Stretch out long from fingertips to toes while at the same time pulling the abdomen up and the waistline down toward the floor. The bottom ribs press down toward the floor so that the spine is flat rather than arched.

33-34	Bend the knees to hook lying position.
35-38	The arms come forward; the head and shoulders come off the floor; at the same time the upper and lower torso carefully roll up to sitting position – one vertebra after the other – slowly coming off the floor, with the waistline pressing down into the floor as you do so.
39-40	Sit forward over your hips, extending the torso and straightening the back as much as possible. Press the top of the head toward the ceiling and stretch the spine up.
41-42	Straighten the legs in front on the floor.
43-44	Bend the torso forward over the legs; touch hands to feet, if possible.
45-46	Raise the torso and sit up tall, well forward over the hips.
47-48	Bend the knees to hook sitting position.
49-96	Repeat counts 1-49. If this movement is uncomfortable for your neck, instead of placing your chin on your torso, keep your chin level and focus your eyes on the ceiling.

This is a long exercise; to do it well, start with one portion at a time till you know it then add the next segment. Do counts 1-16, then 1-34, and finally 1-48. Remember that on counts 1-20 the abdomen must be flat. Place your hands under your thighs and hold your thighs, or place the elbows on the floor, if necessary.

FITNESS MINUTES: This exercise is a good one to use at the end of a workout or class as a cooling-off exercise; it has a nice centered, elasticized feeling to it. If you find yourself clamping your teeth together, you want to get rid of that habit. Press your tongue against the gum ridge of your upper teeth and pull up the corners of your mouth. Now your teeth are not clamped and you have a pleasant expression on your face. To make sure that your abdomen is flat, press your belly button back and down into the floor during sit-ups.

NUTRITION HINT: The diet and health guidelines recommended by most researchers and institutes for disease prevention seem to have the same basic suggestions whether they are for the prevention of cancer, Alzheimer's, diabetes, heart disease, obesity or early aging. The American Institute for Cancer Research, for example, suggests eating plenty of vegetables and fruits; choosing a diet rich in a variety of plant based foods; maintaining a healthy weight (which is easier to accomplish if you are not eating sugar calories) and being physically active; consuming only foods which are low in salt and low in fat; no alcohol; and especially, not using tobacco in any form.

****

No. 4-2 – LOW AND HIGH RAISES

Start on your back with the feet close together, not turned out, the feet flexed and the hands under your head with the elbows pressed or relaxed down on the floor.

1	Pull up the thigh of the right leg – think of reaching out under the leg to the flexed heel – and lift the leg up about 2 inches off the floor.
2	Return the right leg to the floor.
3-4	Reverse.
5-16	Repeat 3 times, counts 1-4 – low leg raises.

17-18   Slowly, with pointing feet and a greater extension, take 2 counts to lift the straight right leg as high as you can while at the same time keeping the shoulders and elbows down on the floor and the abdomen and stomach pulled up.

19-20	Lower the right leg slowly; the leg is straight and the toes pointed. The abdomen remains pulled up.
21-24	Reverse counts 17-20.
25-48	Repeat 3 times, counts 17-24 – high leg raises.

If your working knee tends to bend on this exercise, remember to pull up the thigh, reach out toward the heel, then lift the leg.

FITNESS MINUTES: Practicing the warm-ups, steps and routines in this book should make you feel more fit: flatter abdomen, stronger back, bones and muscles, better shape, more stamina, better balance and coordination, ability to relax more easily, feel less stressed and maintain your desired weight. These should all contribute to a greater enjoyment of other activities in which you participate for cross training: swimming, belly dancing, social dancing, yoga, modern dance, fencing, skiing, Alexander technique, etc.

NUTRITION HINT: A small amount of chocolate is a great comfort food; it raises the level of serotonin in the brain. This chemical regulates mood and helps one to relax, which may be why we love chocolate, besides its taste and smoothness. A small piece is enough to produce this result. In the long run, a large portion will not since it has so many calories. A good rule might be to keep it somewhere out of the way, out of view and only take a small piece at a time. However, there are several nutritious low fat foods, like graham crackers, whole wheat bread and whole wheat pretzels that likewise augment the production of serotonin in the brain and do not boast such a high calorie count. See Glossary.

****

No. 4-3 – ARM FLINGS

Start by lying face down, with the hands under your chin and the legs close together, not turned out.

1-2   Lift the upper torso while flinging the arms back. You will get a better stretch through the upper torso, from shoulder to shoulder, if you open the arms forward

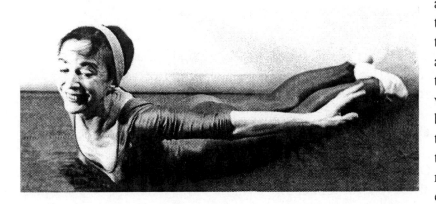

and carry them out to the sides and as far back as they can go while keeping both arms at the height of the shoulders rather than close to the floor.

3-4   Keep the upper torso up as you place the palms on the floor, in front of you, and gently raise the torso slightly more.

5-8   Place the torso down and rest the chin on your hands; relax.

9-32   Repeat 3 times, counts 1-8.

33-40   Relax.

41-80   Repeat counts 1-40.

Remember to pull up the abdomen each time, before lifting up the torso. It will take the pressure off the lower back. The legs are not turned out; the toes remain on the floor; do not raise the torso high at first.

FITNESS MINUTES: If you have a bad lower back you may wish to omit torso raises such as this one. Some people claim this type of exercise strengthens the back and some think it is bad for the back. However, if you tend to get a sore back and you wish to do them, then raise the torso up just a little bit. Be sure to pull in the abdomen; keep the head lined up with your spine; think of lengthening the frontal area; do not tighten the back area. When sitting or lying down place a small pillow behind or under the small of the back to maintain its natural curve.

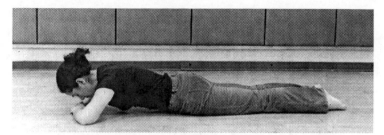

You should also practice the following: Lie down prone, face down, with your chin on your hands, and pull your belly button up off the floor. To do this you'll be pulling your abdomen up and in against your back. This is excellent for your back, and also as a preparation for both of these arm flings, and for straight legged pushups.

There are many other exercises for backs to be found in my book *Aerobic Razzmatazz,* published by 1st Books Library (now called AuthorHouse). Take a look at Nos. 1-3, 1-6, 3-3, 4-7, 8-1 and 12-2 in that book.

NUTRITION HINT: If you follow the suggestions in this book you should not use the word diet to describe what you are eating. You are simply eating nutritious food, packed with vitamins, minerals, antioxidants, and all sorts of good things, while staying away from foods with empty calories, sugar and salt and bad fats. And if you stick to small portions, maybe you can eat just about anything you wish once in a while.

NUTRITION HINT: On the subject of alcohol, according to the American Institute of Cancer Research, it is not recommended for those with a family history of cancer, for pregnant women, or for those allergic to alcohol, but several studies have found that for others, in moderation, a small glass of red wine with dinner is beneficial in lowering the risk of heart disease.

****

No. 4-4 – LEG RAISEBACK

Start on the abdomen, in prone position, with the hands under the chin and the legs close.

1-2   Raise the right leg – straight – with the toes pointing and the hips on the floor.

3-4   Flex the right foot while the leg is still up in back, with both hips down on the floor.

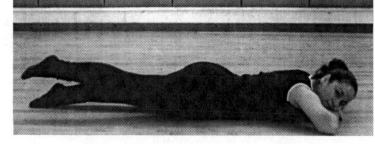

5-6   Point the right foot, with the leg in the previous position.

7-8   Lower the right foot to the floor.

9-16	Reverse counts 1-8.
17-64	Repeat 3 times, counts 1-16, an excellent exercise for the buttocks.
65-72	Relax.
73-144	Repeat counts 1-72.

FITNESS MINUTES: People with back problems need to be aware of how they use their backs in daily activities. When lifting heavy objects, bend the knees; as for carrying objects, close to you and above the waistline is the way to do it; books are best carried on the back, not the side. When carrying groceries, try to equalize the weight between the right and left sides. While vacuuming or shoveling snow, alternate sides; don't bend or twist continually to the same direction; but if you are very right-handed, say, then follow through with some torso twisting to the other side before or afterwards, for better muscle balance. When standing, shift your weight from one leg to the other, with slightly bent legs.

Back pain can result both from insufficient exercise or activity and from over-exercise. But ten or twelve minutes of exercises and dance movements a day should be of great benefit to all backs. Try 8 minutes of the exercises that are done while lying down on the back, then 2 minutes of just relaxing with your back on the floor and your legs bent over a chair seat, if you tend to have backaches, and place a pillow under your lower back.

Other causes of back pain have been found to be extra weight and a sedentary lifestyle. I'll repeat that 10 minutes of flat-on-the back exercises daily, and only bent-knee sit ups would be good for you. (Omit straight-legged ones.)

When you are standing, never lean into the small of the back; pull up from the very bottom of your abdomen, near the legs. Pull your belly button up, back and in toward your spine, as though putting on a pair of tight blue jeans, then pull up the bottom of your breastbone in the middle, so you get your weight up and off your back. Do the same while you sit down; think up. And while you're at it, roll your shoulders up and let them hang down in back, relaxed; then pull the back of your ears and spine up to the top of your head, with your chin just slightly raised. Now, look around with your head resting comfortably on your neck. Doesn't that feel good? Probably looks great, too.

NUTRITION HINT: A positive approach is important for any change of eating habits. Acknowledge when you have gone back to your old ways, but then give yourself approval for attempts at improvement.

NUTRITION HINT: People who are more sensitive to the harmful effects of salt, such as those with diabetes, kidney disease, hypertension, the elderly, and others, need to be especially careful about their salt intake. Reading labels on food cans and packages, buying low-salt canned vegetables, and limiting the consumption of olives, pickles, potato chips, etc., are essential.

****

No. 4-5 – STRETCH AND YAWN

Stand with the arms down at the sides; feet slightly apart and parallel.

1-4   Stretch the arms overhead, with hands in fists that gradually reach out to become jazz hands. The body extends upwards as in a nice, relaxed yawn. The head drops back.

5-8   The body bends forward to flatback position, parallel to the floor, with the arms alongside the ears and the hands in jazz hand position. If this is too difficult, place your hands on the front of the thighs at first.

9-12   Drop the torso down and relax. The back of the neck relaxes and the head drops down. The arms hang down from the shoulders.

13-16   Reach forward to a flatback position, parallel to the floor, with the arms again alongside the ears and the hands stretched into jazz hands, as in counts 5-8.

17-20   Stand up tall with the arms reaching overhead. The weight is still forward.

21-24   Relax the arms down at the sides.

25-96   Repeat 3 times, counts 1-24.

Doing jumps on 2 feet or running in place can be a more challenging version of this exercise, once you've learned it. However, try this later on near the end of your workout, not right at the start. You could even continue doing it, gradually more slowly, and without jumps, as a cooling-down movement.

FITNESS MINUTES: This exercise begins with a stretch, as though you were yawning and stretching on first arising. Yawning is an excellent method for relaxing the throat, neck and shoulders. It's also a good remedy for a tension headache. See if it works for you.

NUTRITION HINT: While attempting to eat healthier foods, containing less fat and sugar, try not to get carried away into devouring more and more of those healthier, lower calorie foods or you'll find yourself gaining weight. A double or triple portion of low calorie, low fat cake, ice cream or whatever, will result in a lot of calories being consumed and turning into body fat on you. Which is why some people are eating healthier meals but are getter fatter. Eat only one serving. Many package labels tell you exactly what consists of one serving size for that particular food.

****

DANCE ROUTINE – COOKIE JAR JUMP

Put on some bouncy, rhythmic music – "Shimmele, Shimmele Ko Ko Bop," or Wang Chung's recording of "Let's Go," or any of your favorites. Walk through the routine for 1-2 minutes; then run through it several times, also, for about 2 minutes.

It will take 32 counts to make a square pattern with 8 counts for each side of the square.

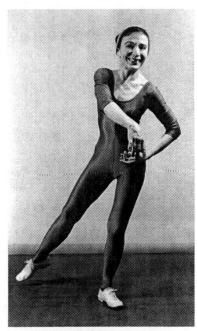

1	Step to the side on the right foot. At the same time the left hand reaches over to the right, as though dipping into a cookie jar to get the last cookie.
2	Step next to the right foot with the left foot. At the same time the left hand comes in to the side of the waist in a fist.
3-6	Repeat 2 times, counts 1-2.
7+	Rock back on the heels as the toes come off the floor, and the arms extend forward, straight, with the palms up and the hands wide open. Then bend the knees as the toes return to the floor and the hands return to their position at the sides of the waist, in loose fists.
8+	Repeat counts 7+.
9-16	As you repeat counts 1-8, make a 1/4 turn to your right to face the other side of the square pattern that this routine follows.
17-64	Repeat 2 times, counts 9-16, to finish the square design to the right side by count 32; reverse counts 1-32 to perform a square to the left.

65-128	Same idea as in counts 1-64, but now with a jump as follows: traveling toward the right, jump sideways onto the right foot with the left leg extended out to the side. Then jump sideways onto the left foot, but next to the right foot. The arm movements remain the same as on counts 1-6. Instead of the

heel rocks of counts 7-8, do 2 jumps on two feet, just plain, and using the same arm movements as before. As in counts 1-32, do a square to the right, then, as in counts 33-64, do a square to the left.

129-   Continue the routine for 2-4 minutes, either walking or jumping through it.

FITNESS MINUTES: People whose ankles and feet tire or swell from having their weight on them for long periods of time, should try to find a moment to relax their extremities by keeping their feet raised higher than their hips; place the calves on the seat of a chair as you rest your hips and upper torso on the floor. Dance students often like to relax on their back, with legs raised, and feet up against the wall for a few minutes; it varies the circulation from the usual standing position. Also excellent for the feet and ankles are a change of shoes, a footbath, a foot massage, or just a few foot exercises; low leg brushes on the floor, foot circles, or clenching and stretching the toes wide are good ones.

NUTRITION HINT: The Asian diet – that of China, Japan, Korea, India, Thailand and Vietnam – is made up of rice, noodles, breads, grains and lots of vegetables such as bok choy, and mushrooms, as well as beans, nuts, seeds, some fish, eggs, poultry and, at times, meat. This diet has little saturated fat and as a result cholesterol levels are low and so the risks of cancer and heart disease are reduced. Soy foods, fish, and tea also help to make the Asian diet such a healthy one. The Human Nutrition Research Center on Aging at Tufts University had only one recommendation, the addition of some low fat milk and cheese for calcium from dairy, to improve bone density.

****

SUGGESTED READING

Christensen, Alice, founder American Yoga Assn. *The American Yoga Association's Beginner's Manual.* NY: A Fireside Book, published by Simon & Schuster, 2002.

Sherbon, Elizabeth. *On the Count of One: Modern Dance Methods.* Palo Alto, California: Mayfield Publishing Co., 1975.

Thomas, David Q., Ph.D. and Nicki E. Rippee, Ph.D. *Is Your Aerobics Class Killing You?* Chicago, Illinois: a cappella books/Chicago Review Press, Inc., 1992.

Vincent, L. M., M.D. *The Dancer's Book of Health.* Mission, Kansas: Sheed Andrews and McMeel, Inc., a subsidiary of Universal Press Syndicate, 1978.

CHAPTER 5 - ROOSTER STRUT

No. 5-1 – Flatback and Relax

No. 5-2 – Round Up – Accent Down

No. 5-3 – Chicken Wings

No. 5-4 – Back Strengthener

No. 5-5 – Curl Up

Dance Routine – Rooster Strut

Suggested Reading

No. 5-1 – FLATBACK AND RELAX

Stand with the feet slightly apart and parallel.

1-4 Raise the arms; at the same time extend the torso forward to a flatback position. The torso is parallel to the floor, like the top of a table. Press your buttocks and thighs together and pull them up, rather than just relaxing them, especially if you have a wide hip and thigh girth and wish to prevent it from getting wider. You may wish to practice this while holding onto a barre or solid furniture before doing the entire exercise if a flatback position is still difficult for you.

5-8 Bend the knees and drop the torso, head and arms down in front; relax the back of the neck.

9-12   Slowly, vertebra by vertebra, roll the torso up to a straight standing position. The arms are down at the sides as you straighten up; then they go overhead as you stretch up more.

13-48   Repeat 3 times, counts 1-12.

49-56   Relax.

57-112   Repeat counts 1-56.

FITNESS MINUTES: Now that you've been enjoying doing fitness workouts it's time to reconsider your alignment and find out whether you need to make any further improvements. People who look like a skinny "S" from the side (chest caved in and hips ahead) should put their weight over the balls of the feet and align the body in a diagonal line going frontward from the base of the feet to the top of the head. Stretch forward with the arms overhead and try to reach high up at a wall in front of you. Drop the arms. All you need to do now is to keep lengthening the spine all the way up through the back of the head, with the chin and the head level. Two other wonderful exercises for better alignment are the Wall/Tummy Flattener, No. 4-7, and the Cat Stretch, No. 3-3, from my book *Aerobic Razzmatazz,* published by 1st Books Library (now called AuthorHouse).

NUTRITION HINT: People who taste food unnecessarily (and thus eat more calories) as they prepare dinner or dessert, and perhaps, as it happens, have become completely unaware of this, should try singing or reciting the words of a song, poem, or joke (humor and laughing are excellent for one's health), keeping the words handy so they can refer to them; mental aerobics, too, is good for one's well-being; otherwise chew on some sugarless gum.

****

No. 5-2 – ROUND UP – ACCENT DOWN

Stand with the feet slightly apart and parallel. Loose fists are at the hips with the palms facing up.

1-3   Rotate the left arm in, the left shoulder forward, and slowly raise the left arm overhead through the front, with first the shoulder, the rounded and slightly bent elbow, then the wrist leading the movement as the arm goes higher. It is a smooth, continuous movement that goes up only three quarters of the way. The right shoulder is back.

+   Quickly continue the upward movement by rotating the arm in an outward direction, thus causing the fingertips to lift way up high, with the elbow facing forward, then down.

4   Quickly lower the arm – elbow leading and pulling the arm down and going back at waist level – so the loose fist is again on the hip with the palm facing up.

5-8   Reverse counts 1-4.

9-32   Repeat 3 times, counts 1-8.

33-40   Relax.

41-80   Repeat counts 1-40.

As the left arm goes up in front with the shoulder forward, the right side of the upper torso will tilt slightly down toward the right and back, with the chest raised high.

Try the above arm movements with an oppositional knee raise to the front – when the right arm moves, the left knee comes up – or try it while doing prances in place. Or do prances forward, backward or to the side, as desired.

FITNESS MINUTES: Music dictionaries occasionally mention that jazz music has a forward-going pulse to it. Well, a dancer's alignment – any dancer – jazz, ballet, social dance, modern dance or tap – is the same; it has a forward-going look: The line goes on a slight frontward diagonal from the heels to the top of the head, with an awareness of having the head lined up over the balls of the feet. I mention dance because so many of us watch dancers on TV or stage shows or like to dance ourselves and are aware of the excellent posture performers usually possess. Well, with a bit of effort yours can be excellent, also.

NUTRITION HINT: Eat smaller portions. Rather than eating large meals, eat four small meals per day. Try to avoid empty calories like sugar. (It has been found by researchers at the New York University School of Medicine that elevated levels of blood sugar may harm memory.) Make each calorie count in nutritional value and in enjoyment. Remember to consume only the *good-for-you* fats – those found in foods such as nuts, peanut butter, olive oil, and many varieties of fish. A blend of complex carbohydrates (fruits, vegetables, and grains), proteins and dairy with good fat only, is best, even for those who are cutting down on food. The combination of proper diet and exercise will result in the most permanent weight loss (and will also help keep blood sugar levels down). The calories are used up while you work out. The food portions are nutritious and small or normal size, not large. If you consume only carbohydrates, then you miss out on the nutritious properties of proteins; if you eat only proteins you leave out all the phytonutrients that are produced by plants. If you omit fat, then fat soluble vitamins can't be absorbed.

****

No. 5-3 – CHICKEN WINGS

Stand with the hands in loose fists at the sides of the waist, with elbows toward the back.

+   Bring the shoulders forward while moving the elbows sharply toward the front of the body, with the fists remaining on the hips at the waist, close to the sides of the body.

1   Press the shoulders back as the elbows move toward the back of the body, loose fists remaining at the sides of the hips with the palms facing up.

+2-16   Repeat 15 times, counts +1.

17-24   Relax.

25-72   Repeat 2 times, counts 1-24.

FITNESS MINUTES: If you have been practicing just the plain version of the steps and routines, please bear in mind that aerobic exercise or dance is any continuous, nonstop movement. Perform the steps and routines many times, without pausing, and you'll be doing more aerobic movement. This is excellent for improved circulation, increased energy and heart fitness. You should also practice the arm movements with some steps or simple jumping movements.

NUTRITION HINT: There's an interesting new food rule developed to get people to eat in a healthy manner without devouring a favorite food and neglecting other nutritious items. You plan your meals and snacks so you eat something from each of 3 groups of food, one of which must be protein. The other groups are fruits and vegetable, dairy, and whole grain. This is the 3-food rule developed by a nutrition counselor, Karen Beerbower. If you are hungry enough to want more of one of the food items, then if you are following the rules, you must take more of all three, not just your favorite. A combination, like stew, salad, sandwich, soup, etc., counts as one item. And, coincidentally, many of the people she was counseling not only ate healthier snacks and meals, but lost weight.

****

No. 5-4 – BACK STRENGTHENER

Start by lying flat on the floor on your abdomen, with the hands on your head.

1-2   Pull up the abdomen and lift the upper torso, head, and elbows off the floor. Inhale.

3-4   Extend the arms forward alongside the ears. Breathe normally. Exhale.

5-6   Hold the upper torso and head off the floor as in counts 3-4 while placing the hands on the back of the head. Inhale.

7-8   Lower the head, torso and elbows to the floor and relax. Exhale.

9-32   Repeat 3 times, counts 1-8.

33-40   Relax.

41-80   Repeat counts 1-40.

FITNESS MINUTES: As you work harder to raise the torso, arms and head slightly more, be sure neither to get tense nor to hold your breath. Try humming, singing to yourself, reciting nursery rhymes, the alphabet and numbers – or work out more slowly. It does help, and you will be able to do the exercise equally well and in a more relaxed fashion. Concentrate on breathing as continuously as you normally do. Look through the various breathing and relaxation exercises and hints found in this book if these are areas that you need to improve. Also check the Index at the back of the book.

NUTRITION HINT: Years ago there was a theory that in the not so distant future humans would no longer sit down for a meal and eat food; they would simply swallow a few pills to provide them with nourishment. But this will probably never happen; the body needs real food. If you enjoy finding new recipes, check the library, bookstores, magazines, television, the Internet and the Bibliography at the end of this book for marvelous, tasty recipes, and many of them for easy-to-make meals. I've read every cookbook in the Bibliography and have found excellent recipes in all of them. If you have an old family favorite that you consider luscious – one with fats, flour, ten eggs, etc., several of these books have suggestions on how to modify these ingredients for a healthier but still delicious recipe, e.g., olive oil for butter, etc., or use the original recipe, make just half of it, eat a small portion and put some in the freezer.

****

No. 5-5 – CURL UP

Start from whatever position you were in at the end of the previous exercise – probably lying down prone.

1-4   Curl up and sit on your heels, with the torso bent down in front. The head is on your knees or as close to them as possible. The arms are either in front, on the floor, alongside your head or in back close to your feet, whichever is best for you.

5-64   Remain in the above position as you also concentrate on relaxing your hips, buttocks, neck, back and thighs. As you do so, you should be able to sink farther down, closer to the floor, if not today, then eventually.

FITNESS MINUTES: This is an excellent position in which to relax, especially after doing any of the exercises with straight leg raises to the back, or with an upper torso raise. This position is relaxing for the entire body. If your feet get sore, try placing a small towel or cushion under them.

FITNESS MINUTES: Concentrating on what you are doing and finding a time and place suitable for better enjoyment of the activity is essential. Remember to do a well balanced workout, with warm-ups for strength, stretch, relaxation, isolations, dance steps, continuous movements – then do it more quickly and non-stop – followed by a relaxing cooling down with slower movements at the end of the activity session.

NUTRITION HINT: Vegetarians are probably successful at eating a variety of 9 fruits and vegetables per day, but the Vegans, who are total vegetarians and eat no dairy, have to think about what is replacing the usual protein. Grains, soy, beans and nuts are excellent in providing the necessary amino acids. A daily multivitamin with 100% of the required B-12 can replace its usual source in meat. Iron from meat is more accessible to the body than iron from vegetables. However, a meal combining a vitamin C source such as tomatoes, oranges or lemon juice with spinach or beans would enable the vitamin C to release the iron in the spinach or beans so the body can make use of it. This is one of the attributes of vitamin C. As for calcium, although easily obtained from dairy, it is found in tofu, legumes and green leafy vegetables – kale, broccoli and bok choy – as well as meat and dairy.

****

DANCE ROUTINE – ROOSTER STRUT

Put on a rhythmic music selection, perhaps from a CD of music to dance to, such as "Ultra Dance Various" – RCA Victor #AFL 1-5322, or Billboards Top Dance Hits or Billboards Top Latin Hits. Go through the routine for 3-4 minutes – walking through it, then gradually running through it; repeat this many times. Do it all in place, or traveling in space if space is available. Start with loose fists at sides of hips with palms facing up.

1-4	Do 4 runs in place, or traveling, lifting the knees up in front. At the same time the rounded right arm goes up with the elbow leading the movement, and then comes down with the elbow again leading the movement. (See No. 5-2.)
5-8	Reverse counts 1-4.
9-16	Repeat counts 1-8.
17-18	Do 2 jumps with the feet apart sideways. At the same time bring the elbows and shoulders sharply toward the front with the loose fists remaining at the sides of the waist. (See No. 5-3.)

19-20	Now do 2 jumps with the feet together and the elbows moving toward the back. (See exercise No. 5-3, Chicken Wings, in this chapter.)
21-32	Repeat 3 times, counts 17-20.
33-48	Repeat counts 1-16.
49-64	Do 8 stride jumps – feet apart and together, 8 times. At the same time bring both rounded arms overhead, but through the sides this time, as you do 2 stride jumps in 4 counts. Then bring the rounded arms down through the sides with the elbows leading the movements, again in 4 counts, as you do 2 stride jumps. Repeat the arm movements for the next 4 stride jumps.
65-	Repeat the routine from the beginning for 2-4 minutes, walking and running through it.

When walking through the routine, instead of doing stride jumps on counts 17-32, step to the side on the right foot with the knees bent then pulse down from the knees 2 times; step in place next to the left foot with the right foot, and reverse. Repeat this same walking sequence for counts 33-64. Then return to the original jumping sequence of counts 1-64, followed by again walking through the routine and so on till the end of the music.

FITNESS MINUTES: A reminder: Cooling down after strenuous jumps and movements is very important in order for the blood flow to return to normal. It is also important in any dance and exercise activity. The cooling-down time can be a review of a centered type of step. It could be a good opportunity to practice arm movements more slowly and fully, or to do some of the opening warm-ups again, more correctly and slowly.

NUTRITION HINT: To cut down on fats, which are the most concentrated source of energy (calories), try some of the following: use water packed sardines or tuna instead of oil packed; put mustard or salsa on your baked potato instead of butter; if you have a yearning for French fries for dinner, have them, but then do not use oil on your salad, use mustard and herbs; use ketchup or mustard on sandwiches instead of margarine, use a little broth or water instead of oil for your stir fry.

NUTRITION HINT: When shopping, read the labels on the food package. The first item listed in the ingredients is the one of which there is the greatest amount. For example, if you are buying a can of whitefish for your cat, and it lists meat by-products before the whitefish, then there is more of that. If you buy a whole wheat bread and it lists enriched wheat flour, then that is what's in the bread, not whole wheat. You have to decide which ingredient

you want, and buy the item containing that as the first ingredient in the listing if possible. Whole-wheat flour has the most nutrients; wheat flour, multigrain, and enriched wheat or white are not as good for you, but if they contain seeds, grains or nuts, that's a plus.

****

SUGGESTED READING

Andreu, Helene. *Aerobic Razzmatazz: 12 Workouts By 12 Minutes Each.* Bloomington, Illinois: 1st Books Library (http://www.authorhouse.com), 2000.

Bauer, Joy, M.S., R.D., C.D.N. *Cooking With Joy.* NY: St. Martin's Press, 2004.

Beerbower, Karen, R. D. *Setting Places.* Maitland, Florida: Nutritional Guidance, Inc., 2000.

Ragone, RD, Regina. "Family Table – Bliss in a Bowl." *Prevention,* October, 2003, Pgs. 148-156A.

CHAPTER 6 - SOUSA JUMP

No. 6-1 – TILT AND SHIFT

Stand with the feet slightly apart and parallel, flat palms (thumbs included) on groin in front, where the thighs and hips join.

1-2	In a rounded shape, with the elbow and wrist slightly flexed, the right arm moves overhead through the front, then out to the right side as the upper torso tilts toward the right side.
3-4	Straighten the torso, reaching up with a long spine whose line extends to the top of the head. At the same time extend the right arm straight out to the side, with the palm facing down.
5-6	Shift the ribcage to the side, moving it directly toward the right side, and reaching out with the bottom ribs as well as with the top ones.
7-8	Return the ribcage to center. At the same time place the flat right palm on the groin in front.
9-16	Reverse counts 1-8.
17-32	Repeat 2 times, the movements in counts 1-16. They will now be executed twice as quickly as before.
33-64	Repeat 1 time counts 1-32.
65-72	Rest.
73-144	Repeat counts 1-72.

If you find the ribcage shift of counts 5-8 difficult, try to do it while sitting cross-legged on the floor or while sitting on a chair. You'll find it much easier, because the hips won't budge; you'll have a very stable base from which to move your ribs. As you shift your ribs to the right, press your left seat or buttock down into the floor and vice versa. Now practice it while standing and continue to practice it first while sitting and then while standing till it is easier for you.

58

Remember that in this exercise, when the right arm moves, the torso moves to the right. The bending and shifting movements occur above the waistline; the hips and thighs do not budge; the hips do not press out to the opposite side; they pull up, as you isolate the upper torso.

FITNESS MINUTES: Relaxation can be achieved through activity, relaxation techniques such as meditation, and also through lying down and going limp or listening to music. For cooling-down purposes, however, it is essential to move at a slower pace than during the workout. If you intend to catnap to relax, cool down by moving slowly before your catnap.

NUTRITION HINT: Variety is the answer if the bad fats or carbohydrates are the ones you prefer. Eat those occasionally, but not too often, say once a month, and eat the good, or better-for-you carbohydrates and fats more often. This way you won't feel completely deprived of your favorite foods and you'll be taking care of your health as well.

****

No. 6-2 – TWINKLE STARS

Stand with the arms down at the sides.

1-2   Spread the fingers of both hands into jazz hand position – very wide hands. Bring the right hand forward and the left one back. The front elbow is bent in at the side, close to the body, and the back elbow is lifted sharply up in back. Now do twinkle stars – shake the hands very rapidly so hands move up and down at the wrists, from pinky to thumb.

3-4   Reverse – bring the left hand in front, the right hand in back, and twinkle – shake jazz hands rapidly.

5-16   Repeat 3 times, counts 1-4.

17-24   Rest the arms and hands.

25-72   Repeat 2 times, counts 1-24.

FITNESS MINUTES: When you are experienced at doing this arm and hand movement, practice it with a low-level passé walk forward, with the opposite hand coming forward and twinkling: The right foot lifts at the side of the left bent leg, with the foot pointing, and then slides in front along the floor. Then reverse the legs and arms and continue stepping forward in this manner. Later try it while moving in a figure eight, or some other numerical, geometrical or alphabetical floor pattern and add a skip.

NUTRITION HINT: Carbohydrates are good for you, but there are the good ones and the bad ones. The good ones are fruits and vegetables with high fiber content, also grain bread like whole wheat, and non-sugared cereals such as oatmeal and all-bran, and brown rice or barley. These are from a plant source, contain few calories, get digested and absorbed so slowly by the body that, in the meantime, the stored fat is used for fuel and energy. Consequently, these good carbohydrates do not cause a gain in weight like the bad ones do. (The Framingham research study found that men were less likely to get osteoporosis if their diet was high in fruits and vegetables.) The bad ones are sugar, white bread, white flour, cake, cookies, the sugary soft drinks, potato chips and other processed foods that don't have worthwhile nutrients. These are high in calories, are absorbed and digested quickly, and can raise the glucose content of the blood rapidly. This sugar gets burned quickly, causes fat to get stored and results in a weight gain, which may then raise the blood cholesterol and triglycerides levels, increasing the risk of heart disease and diabetes. Try to indulge in those only occasionally.

****

No. 6-3 – HIP RELAXER

Start on your back – supine – in hook lying position, with the arms in a wide U overhead; elbows, shoulders, head and hands are down on the floor.

1-2	Turn out the right leg from the hip and place the thigh and knee down as close to the floor as possible without disturbing the other hip.
3-4	Return the right knee to center position, as at the start.
5-8	Reverse counts 1-4.
9-16	Repeat 1 time, counts 1-8.
17-18	Turn out the right leg and place the right knee and thigh on the floor, allowing the other hip to move if necessary.
19-20	Now turn out the left leg and place the left knee out on the floor over to the left side, while keeping the right leg as turned out as possible.
21-22	Roll over enough to place the right turned out knee and thigh on the floor on the right side with the left leg remaining as turned out as possible.
23-24	Roll over and place the left turned out knee and thigh on the floor on the left side with the right knee remaining as close to the floor as possible.
25-32	Repeat 2 times, counts 21-24.

33-36	Straighten the legs, with the feet flexed, and raise the head up while keeping the shoulders and arms down on the floor.

37-40	Return head to the floor and keep the jaw relaxed.
41-48	Repeat counts 33-40.
49-96	Reverse counts 1-48.
97-192	Repeat counts 1-96.

The head raise in counts 33-36 is excellent for the shoulders and upper back, especially if you tend to be at all round shouldered.

You may prefer doing this section with the knees bent if it is more comfortable for your back.

FITNESS MINUTES: To insure that all areas of the body are getting a more complete workout, do some cross training and indulge in a varied exercise program. For example, go swimming, do water exercises, ride a bicycle, or learn some tap dancing or learn some jazz dance steps, isolations and routines from my jazz dance book, *Jazz Dance Styles and Steps for Fun* (it received a 5-STAR review from *Midwest Book Review* as well as from *ForeWordreviews.com)* that was published by 1st Books Library (now called AuthorHouse). Give yourself 2-3 different kinds of workouts each week, once you're used to working out regularly. Boredom won't set in, the variety will keep more parts of your brain active, and you'll have a great time. If you have children, nieces, nephews or grandchildren, occasionally do some of your workouts with them, if it's appropriate for their age.

NUTRITION HINT: People are living longer than ever, so healthy eyes are of importance. Eat your spinach, as mother used to say. And also eat lots of other foods containing the antioxidant lutein, a yellow pigment disguised by chlorophyll in plant leaves to look green. It is found in corn, egg yolks – chickens eat corn – and in green leafy vegetables such as spinach, kale, Brussels sprouts, collard greens, and broccoli, among others. Research has found lutein to help prevent macular degeneration and cataracts. It may also help prevent clogged arteries and arthritis. Lutein is the "in" oxidant right now as far as your eye health is concerned. Also important for eye health is vitamin C, vitamin E, zeaxanthin, beta-carotene, and zinc. See the Glossary for sources of these antioxidants. They are best for you when eaten directly from the foods that contain them.

****

No. 6-4 – FRONT EXTENSION

Start flat on your back, with the arms overhead on the floor in a wide U. The legs are straight and close together.

1-2   Lift the right leg up straight in front with the foot pointed. The abdomen pulls in; the shoulders remain down on the floor.

3-4   Lower the right leg.

5-8   Reverse counts 1-4.

9-16   Repeat counts 1-8.

17-20   With the knee bent, lift the right leg close to the chest and hold the flexed foot at the heel with both hands. At the same time lift the head and round the upper torso.

21-24   Extend the right leg on the floor and flatten the back. The arms return to their position on the floor, overhead, in a wide U.

25-32   Reverse counts 17-24.

33-48   Repeat counts 17-32.

49-96   Reverse counts 1-48.

97-192   Repeat counts 1-96.

Be sure to keep the hips even as you do this exercise, so neither one of the hips is higher than the other.

FITNESS MINUTES: If your quadriceps (the front thigh muscles responsible for controlling the kneecap movements) tend to get tight, stretch them out a bit: Hold onto something solid for balance as you raise your bent right knee in front; hold onto the foot or ankle and gently pull it up in back as close to your buttock as is comfortable. Hold this position for twenty to thirty seconds, relax, reverse, repeat one or two times. If this is difficult for you, lift the foot and hold it up in back with a large towel or belt; otherwise place the top portion of the toes in back of you on the second or third step up as you hold on to the banister, and count to 25, slowly; then change legs. You may bend the standing leg to get a bit more stretch through the leg that is on the stair.

NUTRITION HINT: Read the food labels on products carefully. A can of tuna fish may say 60 calories per serving, but if it claims to contain 2 1/2 servings and you eat all of it, you'll have consumed 150 calories, not 60. It's the same for a box of cookies or a jar of nuts. Food labels also tell you which vitamins or minerals are in the product, and how much sodium (salt), and sugar it contains. The list of ingredients will tell you if it has any partially hydrogenated fats, or high fructose corn syrup – which are not good for you – and whether the wheat in the bread is whole wheat grain, which is the best, or just enriched wheat. Low carb bread may be substituting sugar alcohols like maltitol, sorbitol, or lactitol for sugar, but have as many calories as the plain bread. If you are trying to lose weight, check the label for the number of calories. It's the calories you eat but don't use up in movement that put the weight on you.

****

No. 6-5 – TORSO AND THIGH STRENGTHENER

Start by lying down on the side, with the legs straight and the feet flexed. One arm is under the head and the other is on the floor, in front, for support.

1-2	Raise the top leg just a few inches as the abdomen pulls up against the back. The legs are not turned out; they reach out to the heels.
3-4	Lower the leg.
5-16	Repeat 3 times, counts 1-4.

17-18   Raise the top leg a few inches above the other leg. At the same time lift the upper torso. The hand that is under the head also comes up as the head and upper torso come up; the abdomen pulls up. Relax the shoulders and neck.

19-20   Lower the upper torso, but leave the top leg raised, with the foot still flexed.

21-32   Repeat 3 times, counts 17-20. The spine is relaxed and long; the abdomen is pulled up.

33-34   With the top leg still raised a few inches, lift the bottom leg up to it.

35-36   Lower the bottom leg only.

37-48   Repeat 3 times, counts 33-36.

49-52   Shake out the legs and relax. Prepare to reverse the exercise.

53-104   Reverse counts 1-52.

105-208 Repeat counts 1-104.

If your thighs gets sore from this exercise, sit on the floor and cross your bent right leg over the straight left leg, without turning them out; twist the upper torso to the right side. The right knee points up toward the ceiling and the right foot is flat on the floor. Hold the position for twenty seconds, then reverse.

FITNESS MINUTES: This is an excellent exercise for strengthening the side of the hip and leg, the side of the buttocks and the abdominal muscles. Flexibility and strength go hand in hand for proper technique. It is nice to be very flexible, but then one has to have additional strength in the muscles of that area. The exercises and workout should always be geared toward developing both strength and flexibility.

NUTRITION HINT: Carbohydrates are often classified according to how quickly they cause the blood sugar to rise after being eaten. Those with the highest glycemic index are usually highly processed, such as white bread or white rice, and are digested and changed to glucose rapidly. Normal (fasting) blood glucose is 100 milligrams per deciliter of blood. People with pre-diabetic levels have between 100 and 125. These are people who will greatly benefit from concentrating on daily exercise, no smoking, and proper low calorie diets without sugary or fatty foods; research has found that this regime greatly decreases their chances of getting diabetes, which they do not yet have.

A diet consisting mostly of foods in the high glycemic group, leading to sudden increases in blood sugar, has been found to increase the likelihood of getting diabetes and heart disease. Whole wheat bread and brown rice have the fiber-rich outer bran that takes longer to digest; their glycemic index is low. These help to control type 2 diabetes. The starch in white potatoes is easily digested so it has a high glycemic index. However, if the food is eaten together with some fat – potatoes cooked stir fry in olive oil – it takes longer to be converted to sugar and get absorbed and will not have as high a glycemic index. Acid content will also slow down the conversion of carbohydrates to sugar to be absorbed by the bloodstream, e.g., potato salad with oil and vinegar dressing, so its glycemic index will not be as high.

Carbohydrates used in stews, salads, sandwiches, or as part of dinner are not eaten alone thus their glycemic index is not usually a problem except perhaps for those who are overweight, have a sedentary lifestyle, or whose genes tend to promote diabetes. People with type 1 – juvenile diabetes – do not make enough insulin in the pancreas and as a result can't absorb sugar. Type 2 diabetes – insulin resistance or adult diabetes – causes blood sugar and insulin levels to stay high long after eating. The extensive demands on the insulin manufacturing cells is exhausting for them and they eventually stop producing insulin. Type 2 diabetes is often linked with high blood pressure, high level of triglycerides, low HDL (good cholesterol), heart disease and cancer. The Harvard School of Public Health recommends eating potatoes only occasionally, and not eating highly processed grains, cereals and sugars. Instead eat whole oats, barley, brown rice, whole-wheat pasta, bulgur, wheat berries, millet, quinoa and hulled barley. Many of these can now be purchased at the grocery store. Eat plenty of fruits, vegetables and whole grains.

****

DANCE ROUTINE – SOUSA JUMP

How about some music by Sousa? Basically this whole routine is a high stepping march with the knees lifted high up in front while either walking or running; then for variety the feet are lifted high in back while either walking or running. The arms used are the Twinkle Stars from this chapter as well as some clapping.

1-4   Start with the left foot. Take three steps to the front with the knees lifted high in front and the hands doing Twinkle Stars front and back with the front arm either in opposition to the raised knee or to the stepping foot, whichever you prefer. Pause after the third step, and while the right knee is raised in front clap the hands in front, either with a plain clap or by clapping as though you were striking cymbals.

5-8   Reverse counts 1-4, still moving forward.

9-16   Same idea as counts 1-8: Knees are still raised in front, but you travel to the back.

17-32   Repeat counts 1-16, but now raise the arms as high as you can for both the Twinkle Stars and the claps and raise the feet high up in back.

33-64   Repeat counts 1-32, but for variety, if space permits, go forward diagonally to the front right corner (downstage right – DSR), and back to the back left corner (upstage left – USL).

65-128	Repeat counts 1-32 to the front; then do counts 33-64 this time to the front left corner (downstage left – DSL) and back toward the back right corner (upstage right – USR), again, if space permits.
129-	Continue doing this routine till the end of the music. First by walking through it to the front and the back, then traveling on diagonals to the front right and the back left corners, then again to the front and back and to the diagonal front left and the back right corners. Now you are ready to run through the routine in this same manner. If you have a long enough piece of music, time and energy, keep repeating it in this fashion for 2-4 minutes. Or continue and now do it very slowly with an emphasis on higher arms and legs for a longer routine. Have fun with it.

FITNESS MINUTES: To strengthen your quadriceps and reduce knee pain, do the following: Sit on a chair, extend the right leg straight out and a bit higher than your seat; hold the position for up to ten or twenty seconds; relax, reverse, repeat five times with each leg. You can also do this exercise while sitting on the floor with straight legs in front and resting your hands on the floor in back, or while lying down supine.

NUTRITION HINT: When shopping for food, look for color. Choose richly colored fruits and vegetables; these have more nutrients. Buy processed tomatoes such as tomato paste and sauce. They contain more of the antioxidant lycopene than raw tomatoes due to the heat used in processing them. This is also true about ketchup. Tomatoes are one of several vegetables found to be better for you cooked than raw. A colorful meal with a variety of richly colored fruits and vegetables is a very nutritious one and it is guaranteed to provide you with a variety of antioxidants; you don't have to know which antioxidant, vitamin or mineral is found in which vegetable, just keep eating many, and a variety. Three to five servings of fruit a day and four to six portions of a variety of vegetables are the recommended quantities; it's easy to attain if your between-meal snacks are fruits and low calorie carrots, celery or red or green pepper slices and your lunchtime sandwiches or soups have vegetables in them. To find out more about specific vitamins, minerals or phytonutrients, check the Glossary.

****

SUGGESTED READING

American Heart Association. *American Heart Association One Dish Meals: over 200 all-new, all-in-one recipes.* NY: Clarkson Potter, 2003.

Andreu, Helene. *Jazz Dance Styles and Steps For Fun.* Bloomington, Illinois: 1st Books Library (http://www.authorhouse.com), 2003.

Joseph, James, Ph.D., Dr. Daniel A. Nadeau and Anne Underwood. *The Color Code – A Revolutionary Eating Plan for Optimum Health.* NY: Hyperion, 2002.

CHAPTER 7 - TRUCKIN' FOR FITNESS

No. 7-1 – Hip Press

No. 7-2 – Kneeovers

No. 7-3 – Side Leg Raise

No. 7-4 – Balance and Knee Raise

No. 7-5 – Pivot Turn

Dance Routine – Truckin' for Fitness

Suggested Reading

No. 7-1 – HIP PRESS

Stand with straight legs, feet slightly apart and parallel; the flat palms, thumbs included, are on the front of the groin – where the hip and thigh join.

1+a2 Lift the right arm up directly through the side – the elbow bends down, the hand goes up with the palm facing out; then the fingers flick out to the side when the hand reaches a high diagonal position. At the same time the hips press to the right, left, right and the left; the knees remain straight.

3 Return the right hand – flat palm – to the groin in front, and center the hips.

4 Pause.

5-8 Reverse counts 1+a2, 3-4.

9-32 Repeat 3 times, counts 1-8.

33-40 Relax.

41-120 Repeat 2 times, counts 1-40.

FITNESS MINUTES: If you tend to have stiff joints, keep moving anyway; this may prevent the stiffness from increasing. Exercise is vital to body health. You need to develop and maintain flexibility, balance, strength and endurance. Besides promoting healthier joints, physical exercise will increase the flow of blood to the brain and reduce stress, depression and hypertension, so it is also excellent for your mental and psychological well-being. You should not do one hour of exercise at a time if you find one hour of exercise too exhausting; five minutes many times a day would be great to relieve the joints from sitting or standing too long at a time, or to relieve mental boredom from a dull activity or from sitting at a computer for too long a stretch. Standing and stretching a bit, maybe every 30 minutes, when working at the computer is a good idea, as is looking away from the computer, up, around, or out the window, and slowly blinking your eyes a dozen times while looking up. The greater your personal repertoire of exercises of all sorts, the better able you will be to find one that suits your needs at any particular time.

NUTRITION HINT: Vitamin C, according to a study by the Boston University Medical Center, is useful in preventing wear and tear on joints and keeping them healthy. It is found in cantaloupes, broccoli, citrus fruits, kiwi, bell peppers, and berries, and is necessary for the building of collagen, which is found in bone and cartilage. Vitamin C is also important for strengthening the immune system, for the absorption of iron in the body, for healing wounds and for helping to protect against narrowing and hardening of the arteries. It used to be said that a surplus of vitamin C was not a problem; it would just be excreted from the body. Now research has shown that an overload of it can be harmful and cause kidney stones. A balanced diet and a multivitamin are not considered excessive, but with the addition of a sports juice, sports bar, fortified cereals, etc., one runs the risk of reacting badly to having taken too much of certain vitamins and minerals. More is not always better.

****

No. 7-2 – KNEEOVERS

Start on your back in hook lying position. The hands are under the head, with the elbows relaxed or pressed down on the floor.

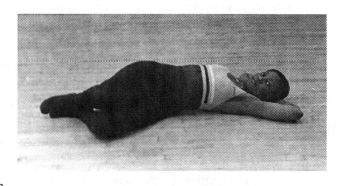

1-2	Both knees go over to the right side, on the floor, with the side of the right foot and knee on the floor and the left foot and knee over them.
3-4	Return the knees to their original position: 2 flat feet on the floor.
5-8	Reverse counts 1-4.
9-32	Repeat 3 times, counts 1-8.
33-34	Both knees go over to the right side, on the floor.
35-36	The top, or left, knee returns to center or slightly past center position; the bottom knee remains on the floor at the side.
37-38	The top knee, the left, now returns to the right side over the right knee.
39-40	Both knees return to their original center position.
41-48	Reverse counts 33-40.
49-96	Repeat 3 times, counts 32-48.
97-192	Repeat counts 1-96.

While doing the kneeovers, try to relax the ribcage down toward the floor and pull the abdomen in against your back. The head should turn and look the opposite direction, away from the knees, to make sure the shoulder is down on the floor. The more you press in your abdomen, the more your back will be able to relax and press down into the floor.

FITNESS MINUTES: Watch the pop music groups; you've probably noticed many of the instrumentalists, as well as the singers, doing a few fancy hops, runs and dance moves on the stage. Dancing has been IN for quite a while, on stage as well as in health clubs and dance studios, where all ages are finding some suitable class to attend – social dance, tango, salsa, belly dancing, tap, ballet and modern. They're excellent activities, and provide recreation, socializing and exercise at the same time; these are wonderful for you both mentally and physically. Join the dance trend; it will provide enjoyable cross training.

NUTRITION HINT: If you are just beginning to get involved in health, diet and fitness, you are not alone. Now more than ever before, people are getting caught up in the trend to participate in dance, exercise and physical movement, but maybe not as much as they should. In the New York City area alone, innumerable health clubs and dance studios are springing up constantly. You can gauge the growth of the physical fitness movement on a nationwide basis by leafing through the pages of catalogues, magazines, and advertisements devoted to apparel, equipment for working out at home or in a studio, health clubs, and dance studios. TV stations are constantly mentioning popular diets and the need for better eating habits; books on the subject are advertised and several are on the bestseller lists. Why? Because men, children and adults are all getting heavier throughout the world and something must be done about this. In the United States a large percentage of the population is more than 100 pounds overweight.

****

No. 7-3 – SIDE LEG RAISES

Start by lying on your left side: the left elbow is on the floor under your shoulder; the forearm and hand are extended in front of you, and the palm is on the floor. The right arm is extended up diagonally. Both knees are slightly bent. The upper torso is raised up off the floor.

1-2   With the right leg bent and turned out, place the sole of the right foot on the floor in front of the other leg. At the same time pull up through the left side so that the left ribs are held in; do not round down toward the floor, causing the shoulder bones to stick out and the torso to slump. To check if you are pulling up, try lifting the hips off the floor. Then when you return the hips to the floor, the body should remain as pulled up through the torso as when the hips were off the floor.

3	Extend the right leg diagonally to the side, low level at first, at the same height at which the thigh was held on counts 1-2. The foot is now pointed.
4	Flex the foot of the raised right leg.
5-7	Lower the straight right leg down to the floor, while still pulling up through the torso. The foot is flexed and the leg reaches out, fully extended, as it slowly goes down to the floor.
8	Relax the right leg.
9-32	Repeat 3 times, counts 1-8.
33-36	Roll over on your back, shake out the legs, and then roll over to the other side and prepare to reverse the exercise.
37-144	Reverse counts 1-36 (counts 37-72); repeat counts 1-72.

As soon as you can easily lift the leg off the floor and do the exercise with the hips on the floor and the torso and ribcage still pulled up, try lifting the leg up just a little higher.

FITNESS MINUTES: This exercise can be extremely frustrating – the more the torso pulls up, at first, the lower the leg goes. But as you persist in doing this exercise and others, the easier it will be to lift your leg correctly, since your strength, flexibility and therefore your extension, will increase. This will also carry over into all your standing extensions.

NUTRITION HINT: The body does not easily absorb vitamin B-12, found in meat, clams, milk and fortified cereals, so a supplement is often recommended even for meat eaters. A multivitamin will supply 100 per cent of the daily requirement of this vitamin, but the Director of the Dietary Assessment Program at Tufts University even suggests an added supplement of 500 micrograms. (For this quantity, which seems quite high, be sure to get your own doctor's approval.) Lack of B-12 can cause fatigue, heart disease and Alzheimer's.

However, as a general rule it's good to read labels and consider the daily requirement of a vitamin, because vitamin A, for example, can cause problems if you take more than you should, and 100 percent of it in a cereal, plus 100 percent of it in a multivitamin and say 100 percent of it in a sports bar and then again in a sports drink would really be excessive. A surplus of vitamin A could lead to fractures, or liver damage, too much calcium to kidney stones or decreased magnesium absorption, too much iron to other problems. So, 100 percent of your daily requirement in a multivitamin supplement is probably all you should take of anything, including B-12, without your doctor's approval.

****

No. 7-4 – BALANCE AND KNEE RAISE

Stand with the feet slightly apart and parallel. Jazz hands are crossed overhead at the wrists and the palms face forward, or use arms as shown in photo.

1   Lift the right leg in front with the knee bent sharply and the foot pointing.

2   Leave the right leg up as it was, but now flex the foot.

3-4   With the leg still bent up, point and flex the foot.

5-6   Point and flex the foot once more, with the leg still up in front.

7-8   Lower the leg.

9-16   Reverse counts 1-8.

17-32   Repeat one time, counts 1-16, with a bent standing leg.

33-64   Repeat counts 1-32.

65-72   Relax, turn out the legs with heels together.

73-136   Repeat counts 1-64, but to the side or somewhat diagonal between side and front, and with a turnout.

FITNESS MINUTES: Once you are familiar with this exercise try it with runs and hops. Do two runs on counts 1-2; hops on counts 3, 4, 5, 6, 7, then run again for count 8. Then on the next 8 counts the movements are reversed; the hops are all on the other foot. Repeat all.

FITNESS MINUTES: As you lift the knee of the working leg, press down and in toward your center at the hip of the working leg, rather than "sitting" on your standing leg, so the hips are parallel to the floor, and not one higher than the other. Pull up from the base of the standing leg, the heel, pressing the weight forward over the ball of that foot, and lifting up through the spine and up to the top of the head. The overhead arm position helps you to pull up through the ribcage. The shoulders should be directly over or slightly in front of the hip line, not in back of the hips. If you tend to lift the hip of the working leg, then press the side of the standing hip against a wall and try to keep it there as you do the exercise; turn around to do the reverse.

NUTRITION HINT: A minimum amount of salt consumption is recommended for most people, except those undertaking very strenuous physical activity for long hours, at extremely hot temperatures. Too much salt (sodium) can cause high blood pressure, as well as a loss of calcium which then increases the risk of osteoporosis. Either rinse canned fish and canned vegetables in water to get rid of excess salt, or buy those labeled low salt or 50 percent less sodium. Also limit foods such as bacon, pickles, olives, sauerkraut, salad dressings, mustard, teriyaki, ketchup, horseradish, Worcestershire and soy sauces. Increase the amount of fresh produce that you use. Do some comparison shopping for deli foods, canned soups, canned fish and vegetables; buy the ones with the lowest sodium content on the label. Don't overeat.

****

No. 7-5 – PIVOT TURN

Stand with the feet slightly apart and parallel; knees are bent; arms are held in at the sides, with the elbows bent toward the back and the hands in loose fists, with the wrists close to the hips and the palms facing forward rather than toward the sides.

+a   No movement, so that the following movement on count 1 will be very sharp.

1   Step back on the ball of the right foot and at the same time do a 1/2 pivot turn to the right so that the right foot is now the front foot and you are facing the back of the room; the weight is mostly forward over the right foot, which is now flat on the floor The head has turned sharply so that it has quickly focused on the back of the room. The heel of the back left foot is off the floor. The shoulders, hips, and knees also face directly to the back, quickly and sharply. There should be no lazy left shoulder or left hip straggling behind, and no turnout in the legs. This is very important, in order to do the same action throughout, without any visible up and down motions.

2	No movement.
+a	No movement.
3	Do a pivot turn to the left, so you end up facing the front of the room again. See count 1 for details.
4	No movement.
5-6	Close the back right foot next to the left foot, with the feet together and parallel and the knees bent.
7-8	Pause.
9-32	Repeat 3 times, counts 1-8.
33-64	Reverse counts 1-32.
65-128	Repeat counts 1-64.

Practice a few jumps with the right foot in front, then with the left foot in front. Do 4 with one foot in front, then 4 with the other foot in front. Now practice the exercise as written, but add a jump to the turn so you turn and jump simultaneously. Be sure to keep the head movements just as sharp as you did on count 1 of the pivot turn.

The pause with no movement on counts +a followed by a very quick turn on the beat adds syncopation and excitement to the turn. Do an extra step at the end to close the feet together.

FITNESS MINUTES: For better mental health, how about some exercise for the brain? Try to learn the words to a song or memorize a joke. Laughing is excellent for one's health. Do a jigsaw or crossword puzzle. Learn a new language with books, tapes and library conversation groups. Take a refresher course of a language or an instrument you once studied. Do some volunteer work at the Botanical Garden, the museum or the library. Catch up on the latest books or maybe on the classics; read the newspaper. Search for a recipe that you might enjoy and try it out. The library, the Internet and magazines are full of marvelous recipes just waiting for you. The Bibliography near the end of this book has a section on cookbooks and includes recent ones with delicious, healthy recipes.

NUTRITION HINT: Potassium is an important mineral in our diet. It helps to reduce blood pressure as well as to limit the possibility of kidney stones and bone loss. It is easily obtained from fresh fruits and vegetables: cantaloupes, spinach, Brussels sprouts, mushrooms, apricots, bananas, oranges, potatoes and grapefruits, as well as peanut butter, dried beans and even coffee, tea and cocoa. Look through the Glossary for other minerals.

****

DANCE ROUTINE – TRUCKIN' FOR FITNESS

An old favorite such as "Yakety Axe" as arranged by Chet Atkins in 1965 for RCA Victor, or a newer selection such as "Dancin' in the Dark" by Bruce Springsteen is suitable for this routine.

1	Kick the right leg diagonally front-side as you snap the fingers of both hands forward.
2-4	Do a grapevine to the left: step back on the right foot, side on the left, and front on the right foot. The knees are bent.
5-8	Reverse counts 1-4.
9-12	Repeat counts 1-4.
13-14	Pivot turn to the left; pause.
15-16	Pivot turn to the right; pause.

17-32 Take 8 steps to make a small individual circle to your left as follows: step on the left foot on the 1st count, then bend the knee and either lift the right knee up in front, or do a small kick to the front; reverse; repeat 3 more times. The right index finger shakes overhead as in the famous 'Truckin' step of the 1920's.

33-64 Reverse counts 1-32; start by kicking the left leg.

65-128 Run through the routine. Instead of the pivot turn, jump as you turn, then jump with one foot in front of the other instead of pausing as you previously did on counts 13-16. Repeat this jumped turn and the jump with the feet apart, front and back. Replace the step and bent-knee-up of counts 17-32 with either 16 running steps in a circle, or with a run and hop, or with a run and small kick front as you hop. These are to be done 8 times in the circular pattern.

129- Continue doing the routine for 2-4 minutes, either walking or running through it as you desire. On each repetition alternate the hands, so you also use the left index finger.

FITNESS MINUTES: Take a few minutes, occasionally, to sit, relax, close your eyes (no, don't fall asleep), breathe slowly, and plan your day. Include in your plan anything that you have to get done; don't omit things you do not want to do. If it has to be done, it goes into your plan, you do it, and then you can relax and forget about it; procrastinating leads to stress. You don't need that.

NUTRITION HINT: For good health your fitness program should include a variety both in your exercises and in your diet. The best diet has foods from the four basic food groups – meat, fish and eggs, dairy products, whole grains, and fruits and vegetables – and includes the diversity to be found within each group. This makes it easy to get the whole assortment of antioxidants, vitamins, minerals, phytonutrients, good fats, etc., without even thinking too much about them. Salt, sugar and animal fats should be kept at a minimum. This does not mean you should deprive yourself completely of your favorite foods. You eat them on an occasional basis instead of indulging in them regularly. And you eat a small portion, not a normal portion. A usual size portion of apple, or banana is a medium one; a portion is 1/2 a grapefruit, 1/4 cantaloupe; 1/2 cup or a tennis ball size of chopped raw or cooked fruit or vegetable; 1 cup of raw, leafy vegetables; a deck of cards is the size for meat, or fish; 6 ounces for fruit, vegetable juice or yogurt; usually its one slice of bread, except for a few thin, small slices; a small scoop of ice cream; and read the labels for the serving sizes of packaged items.

****

SUGGESTED READING

Brody, Jane. *Jane Brody's Good Food Gourmet*. NY: W.W. Norton & Company, 1990.
Gittleman, Ann Louise, L. S., C.N.S. *Get The Salt Out, 50l Simple Ways to Cut The Salt Out of Your Diet*. NY: Crown Trade Paperbacks, 1996.
University of California at Berkeley and the Editors of the Wellness Cooking School. *The Wellness Lowfat Cookbook*. NY: Rebus Inc. Publishers (distributed by Random House) 2003.

CHAPTER 8 - CLAP YO' HANDS

No. 8-1 – STRIDE SITTING AND BENDING

Start in stride sitting position, sitting well forward with the spine extending up in a forward diagonal, the shoulders back and the abdomen pulled up. The buttocks and thighs are both placed firmly on the ground, with the knees facing the ceiling. Place the legs as far out to the sides as is possible while maintaining the correct position.

1-2	Reach up with the right arm.
3-4	Reach up with the left arm.
5-8	Repeat counts 1-4.
9-12	Bend or tilt the torso directly over to the right side, not necessarily over the right leg – with the left arm overhead, and the elbow held back. The head looks up at the left elbow and the right hand is on the floor.

13-16	Bend forward and relax the torso forward, rounded. The hands are on the floor in front. The legs remain straight with the buttocks and thighs firmly on the ground; the knees face the ceiling and are out as far as possible with the correct position.
17-20	Reverse counts 9-12 and bend the torso to the left, with the right arm overhead and the left one on the floor. Bend directly to the side, pressing the opposite hip down on the floor.
21-24	Arms go overhead and then open out and down to the floor in back, close to you, as you arch the torso back. Sit well forward and think of lengthening the front area, pulling in the abdomen, and relaxing the lower back without tightening it and without pressing down into it. The only section of the back that you should feel is the shoulder blades pulling together as the back arches.

25-48	Reverse counts 1-24.

49-144   Repeat 2 times, counts 1-48.

FITNESS MINUTES: Following are a few relaxation techniques to add to your cooling-down exercises: Stand up and take a big breath all the way from the bottom of the abdomen as you raise the arms up; then drop the arms and drop the torso down in front, from the hips.

Or, similar to the previous one, but just standing up tall – breathe in and out slowly; this can be done anywhere and without making a big production out of it. Concentrate on breathing more and more slowly and on relaxing through the entire torso as you do so.

Lie down on your back, arms overhead, and stretch out diagonally from one hand to the opposite leg; then relax and breathe deeply from the abdomen; then reverse the stretch on the other diagonal while pulling in the tummy and pressing the waistline down against the floor. The legs straighten out gradually from the buttocks to the flexed feet.

Sitting down, wherever you are, or lying down, relaxation can be achieved by slowly and gradually tightening one muscle after the other, holding this for 10 to 20 seconds and then relaxing for 10 to 20 seconds before proceeding to the next group, till you have gone through your entire body, more or less. If you lose your concentration, start again.

NUTRITION HINT: As a general rule, after class, it is always a good idea to eat something, to replenish the energy you used during class or during a strenuous workout – maybe some yogurt, a hard boiled egg, or low fat cheese, with a banana or an apple; this should prevent you from feeling fatigue, and your body will more easily maintain your muscles in good repair. And remember to drink water to restore your fluids. Lack of water can make you feel your sore muscles more.

****

No. 8-2 – FLATTER ABDOMEN

Lie down in a supine position – on your back – with your arms close to you at the sides, legs straight, feet together and pointing. The abdomen pulls up and the waistline presses down toward the floor.

1-2   Pull up the abdomen; press the waistline and bellybutton down toward the floor; lift the head, shoulders, and arms up in front. If the abdomen is not flat, do not lift the head up so high. Flex the feet and pull up the thighs with the legs  stretching out from the buttocks to the flexed feet.

3-4   Relax the head, shoulders, and arms down on the floor and point the feet.

5-16	Repeat 3 times, counts 1-4.
17-24	Relax as you press the shoulders down on the floor.
25-72	Repeat 2 times, counts 1-24.

A general rule for breathing during this sort of exercise is to inhale when you relax the abdomen, on counts 3-4, and exhale when the abdomen is pulled up and flattened, on counts 1-2.

When pulling in the abdomen, think of pulling it up toward your head, rather than just squashing it down in place. You'll feel as though it has some place to go as you pull it up.

To relax the legs, raise them up toward the ceiling and shake them out by alternately straightening and bending the knees in this position.

FITNESS MINUTES: There are three kinds of breathing: abdominal, diaphragmatic and thoracic. They are all used at various times, depending on the activity. Abdominal breathing is excellent for relaxation purposes. But there is a good portion of both of the other kinds of breathing going on in daily activities and during movement sequences – depending on the physical need and on the desired bodyline. Since abdominal breathing would involve having a protruding abdomen on each inhalation and also a slower and larger intake of air than is normally required, in dance it is used mainly for specific warm-ups done for relaxation purposes. Thoracic breathing is the shallowest and quickest and would certainly be used if you had just run up two flights of stairs. Diaphragmatic breathing is the happy medium and allows you to use your voice with more expertise, power and range.

NUTRITION HINT: If you have eaten a large meal, a wait of two hours is best before doing strenuous exercise and before lying down. A walk is always excellent even immediately after a meal and is also an aid to digestion.

****

No. 8-3 – SHAKE AND STRETCH

Stand with the arms overhead. Palms face down, and fingers extend out to the sides. The hands hang from the wrists to the fingertips in a long line without any knuckles showing.

1-3	Without moving the arms from their high diagonal position, shake the hands out and toward the back. In other words, the hands move slightly front, then to the back repeatedly.
4	Pause.

5-7	Continue the same hand movement as in counts 1-3, while bending the torso to the right side. The arms remain in the same relative position to the upper torso and head as in counts 1-3. The torso pulls up toward the hands.
8	Pause, with the torso bent to the right side.
9-11	Resume the hand shaking movements of counts 1-3, but return the torso to an upright position.
12	Pause, with the torso in an upright position.
13-16	Reverse counts 5-8.
17-64	Repeat 3 times, counts 1-16.

Notice that the design made by the hands in this step goes out to the side, not in toward the center. This step is marvelous for relaxing the hands and wrists.

Here is a movement that can easily be done while sitting down, to relax the hands and stretch the torso while working at the computer.

FITNESS MINUTES: You have probably noticed as you practiced the exercises, steps, and routines in each chapter that they include a wide variety of movements. For best results a good program of exercise and dance should have this – not all in one day, week, or month – but over a period of time, say a year. And if it's fun, you're more likely to persevere.

NUTRITION HINT: If you are weight conscious, and who isn't with all the talk about obesity being so prevalent all over the world, you might hesitate to snack between meals. But a snack in mid-morning or mid-afternoon is excellent providing it has only a few calories, and it does have some protein, fiber and carbohydrates. Such a snack should curb your appetite and prevent you from overeating for lunch or dinner. Also, your energy level will remain high, allow you to accomplish more and thus use up the calories from the snacks.

Appropriate snacks might include one from each of these groups: fiber – a handful of wheat cereals, 1/2 slice of wheat bread or a graham cracker; carbohydrates – a fresh fruit, maybe 1/2 a large apple, a vegetable: slices of carrots, celery, peppers or a few leaves of green lettuce or spinach; protein – a hard boiled egg, a tablespoon of peanut butter, a slice of turkey or chicken or a small amount of low fat cheese (the consumption of regular cheese, not the low fat variety, is supposed to be the worst culprit in the blocking of arteries). However, if overeating is caused by some emotional problem, then take a short brisk walk, call up a friend, meditate, listen to music or try some of the other relaxation techniques mentioned in this book. See the index.

****

No. 8-4 – SHOULDER CIRCLES

Stand with the hands at the sides of the hips and fingers pointing down.

1+2   The left shoulder moves forward, up, and back in place.

3+8   Repeat 3 times, counts 1+2.

9-16   Reverse counts 1-8.

17-32   Repeat counts 1-16.

33-64   Repeat counts 1-32, but now reverse the direction of the shoulder circles and move the shoulders back, up, forward and in place.

65-72   Move both shoulders together, 4 times, forward, up and back in place.

73-80   Move both shoulders together, 4 times, back, up, forward and in place.

81-160   Repeat counts 1-80.

As either shoulder does the 2 shoulder circles, try to isolate that area completely, so that the rest of the body remains motionless.

Once you've mastered the shoulder isolations add small prances or jumps on two feet.

FITNESS MINUTES: If you are feeling tense, or if your shoulders are tired, or rounded from poor alignment, then it is great for relaxation to do shoulder circles, not as described here but just any old way at first as long as you relax the shoulders: to the front, the back, 1, 2 or 3 times, who cares, just relax them and drop the arms down at your sides, too, if you prefer to do the circles that way. Then some other time you can do them more precisely, as written here.

Not everyone feels tension in the same area. As you read through the Fitness Minutes, look for relaxation hints for the various areas of the body; a well-rounded fitness program should include some that you can turn to when you need them. Take a look at the Index at the end of the book for specific ones.

NUTRITION HINT: Don't ever take megadoses without consulting your doctor since overdoses of certain vitamins and minerals may lead to severe disorders. An excess of vitamin E may increase the risk of heart attacks and strokes; an excess of C may cause nausea, abdominal pain and diarrhea. An excess of A may decrease bone density. Although many authorities in the field do recommend taking an adult multivitamin supplement daily, some recommend that adults take a child's daily multivitamin, with the lower dosages of vitamins and minerals.

A daily multivitamin pill is not considered excessive with a well balanced diet. However, with the addition of a sport drink, sports bar, and a very enriched cereal there may be a dangerous excessive dosage of vitamin A. Anyone eating a dish of such cereals and taking a supplement should bear this in mind.

An interesting fact was found in an 8-year study by Harvard researchers, published in the New England Journal of Medicine They stated that a daily multivitamin, though not a cure for AIDS, was a method of improving and lengthening the quality of life of women with H.I.V. at a minimal cost ($15 per year), especially in poor countries where the necessary drugs are not obtainable. The supplements did not fight the virus but improved the immune system of the individual whether or not they were undernourished.

****

No. 8-5 – ELBOWS UP AND DOWN

Stand or sit with the arms extended out at the sides in jazz hand position, hands stretched wide, with elbows bent and forearms about waist high.

+   Lift the shoulders up, with the arms and hands also moving a bit.

1   Lift the elbows up, almost shoulder height, with the forearms held at approximately a right angle to the upper arms and hanging down from the elbows; the hands are still in jazz hand position but now the fingers point down. At the same time that the shoulders go down in place, they rotate toward the front, and the ribcage shifts back, rounding the upper torso as the shoulders come forward.

+   Lift the shoulders up, moving the entire arms and hands up a bit.

2   Lower the elbows and shoulders, with the forearms and jazz hands returning to the starting position. At the same time the ribcage shifts forward and the upper torso is arched, since the shoulders go back slightly as they come down.

+3-8   Repeat 3 times, counts +1+2.

9-12   Relax.

13-48   Repeat 3 times, counts 1-12.

When you are an expert at this arm movement, try it with stride jumps with feet apart sideways, then together, or with one foot in front and the other in back, then together, alternately.

This is another movement that can easily be done while sitting and that provides a good stretch for the hands and shoulders as well as relaxation for people using computers.

FITNESS MINUTES: As a variation, for balance, and to stretch and strengthen the legs, add this to the arm movement, but do the simple version first. It is excellent even for beginners. With the arms out at the sides and the palms facing up, rise up on the ball of the standing leg with the other leg raised, bent, and its foot pointed and next to the standing leg; clap the hands overhead as you rise up; then open the arms out to the sides as you lower the heel. Do this eight times. Concentrate and don't wiggle; keep your balance, with a long spine, head erect, and shoulders back. Reverse the legs and practice. Now you are ready to try the balancing with the arm movements from exercise No. 8-5. On + you rise and on the counts 1, 2, etc., you lower the heel. However, if this is too easy for you, rise on +1, lower the heel on +2, etc. Have fun. Practice both sides.

NUTRITION HINT: Researchers have found that those who eat nuts or peanut butter regularly are getting many health benefits: a lowered risk of heart diseases, a lowered risk of Type 2 diabetes, as well as a lowering of blood cholesterol levels. As for the hydrogenated fats and trans fats in peanut butter, the USDA research found the amounts to be minimal in peanut butter. Nuts are high in calories, so care should be taken to eat less of other calories. However, nuts are rich in phytochemicals, antioxidants, fiber, vitamin E, minerals like copper, potassium and magnesium, the B vitamins including folate, the good fats such as monounsaturated and polyunsaturated fats. All of these items are linked with promoting a healthy heart, lowering cholesterol, and inhibiting blood clotting.

Instead of snacking on these nutty goodies and gaining weight from all their calories if you eat too many, The Harvard School of Public Health recommends that you add a few chopped or slivered nuts to cereals, cooked vegetables, salad, rice, or yogurt. The unsaturated fats in nuts help to lower the LDL (bad) cholesterol and raise the HDL (good) cholesterol. The omega-3 fatty acids from walnuts (much like the ones in salmon and bluefish) may help prevent blood clots as well as erratic heart rhythms. See the Glossary for the benefits to be obtained from the minerals and vitamins found in nuts.

****

DANCE ROUTINE – CLAP YO' HANDS

"Clap Yo' Hands" is an excellent selection to use with this routine, or try some country music or square dance tune, such as "O, Them Golden Slippers."

1   Jump onto the right foot and place the left heel on the floor to the side, with the toes up off the floor.

2-3   Reverse 2 times.

+4   Hold the previous position as you clap your hands 2 times.

5-8   Reverse counts 1-4.

9-16   Repeat counts 1-8.

17-22   Take 6 running steps in place, medium speed, and tap the side of the free foot with the hand that is on that same side. The other hand counterbalances the movement by going up high at the side.

23   Jump in place with both feet together.

+24   Clap the hands overhead, 2 times.

25-32   Repeat counts 17-24.

33-48   Do 8 pony prances, 2 counts for each, as follows: do a small jump onto the free foot; touch the ball of the other foot on the floor in front; then do a small jump back, in place, on the first foot. Reverse. Repeat 3 times. The hands are held high overhead, diagonally to the sides, and the hands shake toward the back, as in No. 8-3 – Shake and Stretch, from this chapter.

49-64   Now jump backward on 2 feet, 8 times, as you press the palms out on the offbeat – first forward, then overhead toward the ceiling or sky. You would then jump on count 49, and press the palms on count 50, and so on.

65- Continue doing the routine for two to four minutes. Do it in a more relaxed fashion, then more energetically, and so on.

FITNESS MINUTES: Better relaxation is often a beneficial result of participating in an exercise or dance program, but for those who need to consider relaxation by itself, deep breathing can be excellent. Lying on your back with the knees bent, take a few minutes to do the following: Breathe in, letting the abdomen stick out; then exhale. Count to yourself – 4 counts for each inhalation and 4 counts for each exhalation. Gradually breathe more slowly, so each inhalation and exhalation takes up more counts.

NUTRITION HINT: Sardines, canned salmon with bones, tofu, green vegetables – such as broccoli, kale or watercress – and low fat dairy products – such as yogurt and milk – are excellent sources of calcium. If you cannot digest milk, then low fat hard cheeses such as cheddar, Swiss and Parmesan are best. Other good sources are almonds and figs. All of these together with an exercise program help to prevent osteoporosis. Walking, dancing, skating, gardening, pushing the baby carriage, or the shopping cart, all weight bearing standing movements are best. They place stress on the bones, which increases the bone mass after their usual growth has stopped. These foods and weight bearing exercises are beneficial for senior citizens, too.

****

SUGGESTED READING

Fitness Magazine Editors with Karen Andos. *The Complete Book of Fitness.* NY, NY: Three Rivers Press, 1999.

Stephenson, Richard, M. and Joseph Iaccarino. *The Complete Book of Ballroom Dancing.* NY: Doubleday, 1992.

Wellness Letter, The Newsletter of Nutrition, Fitness and Self-Care. University of California, Berkeley, California, 2000-2005.

CHAPTER 9 - LOCOMOTOR EXPRESS

No. 9-1 – Torso and Abdomen

No. 9-2 – Flutter, Stretch and Curl

No. 9-3 – Hinge, Press, Stand

No. 9-4 – Twist and Slim

No. 9-5 – Shrug It Off

Dance Routine – Locomotor Express

Suggested Reading

No. 9-1 – TORSO AND ABDOMEN

Start on your back with legs bent and arms down at the sides, palms facing down.

1-4   Arch the torso; the ribs reach up as the head rolls back and under you, so you have the top of the head on the floor. The weight is on the elbows at the sides of the body; the torso pulls up so there is no weight on the top of the head. Relax the small of the back and press the buttocks into the floor in a relaxed position.

5-8   Straighten the back and return it flat to the floor as you roll off the top of the head.

9-12   Straighten the legs.

13-16   Point and flex the feet, stretching the straightened legs out all the way to the heels and toes, 2 counts for each.

17-22   Sit up, slowly rounding the back and pulling in the abdomen. The feet continue pointing and flexing as you roll up, so the legs are continuously stretching lengthwise as you do so. The hands may remain on the floor to facilitate your rounding the back, keeping the waistline on the floor, and pulling the abdomen in and up, flat.

23-24   Reach well forward beyond your toes, if you can.

25-32   Hands are in front, elbows out. Twist the upper torso to the left and to the right, 2 times.

33-38   Slowly roll down your back, vertebra by vertebra, and place the arms overhead on the floor, with the shoulders relaxed down. At the same time the abdomen has been pulling up and the feet have continued the pointing and flexing movement from before.

39-40   Return the arms to your sides, palms down.

41-160   Repeat 3 times, counts 1-40.

Be sure to press up off the floor on counts 1-4, so you do not place any pressure on the top of the head.

Straight-legged sit-ups such as this one are very good for legs and hips, especially when done with flexing and pointing of the feet. This makes you aware of lengthening through the legs and hips as you do the sit-ups. But do place your hands on the floor if this helps you to take the strain off the back as you roll up and pull in the abdomen. And back pain means you should stick to bent knee sit-ups for a while, or just do one or two of these and with your hands on the floor.

FITNESS MINUTES: If you have a flat abdomen and do not need to keep your hands on the floor to assist you in rounding the back, then either make a fist with the hands, or pulse them by alternately bending and extending them.

NUTRITION HINT: What's the best way to eat vegetables, cooked or raw? Both are excellent. Try them cooked one day and another day raw in a salad, in chunks, or shredded. Spinach, tomatoes, broccoli, green and red peppers, onions, carrots, celery, cauliflower, corn and many other vegetables are very tasty either way. Use them raw and cooked; just eat lots of them.

****

No. 9-2 – FLUTTER, STRETCH AND CURL

Start by lying flat on the floor in a prone position – on your abdomen – feet just slightly apart, lined up with your hips, and hands under your chin.

1-2	Slowly lift the right straight leg off the floor, leaving the hips down on the floor. This is very good for the buttocks.
3-4	Slowly lift the left straight leg off the floor, with the hips down on the floor; at the same time place the right straight leg on the floor. There is a moment in each leg raise when both legs are off the floor.
5-16	Continue the slow leg raising as in counts 1-4.
17-20	Relax with both legs down on the floor.

21-22   Place the hands under the shoulders and raise the upper torso as you look up at the ceiling. Try to press the shoulders back and the chest forward so the shoulders are not forward. Naturally, as in all torso-arching exercises, you pull in the abdomen before beginning the movement.

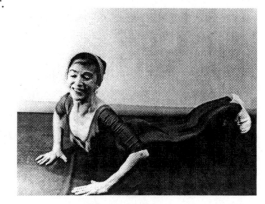

23-24   Place the torso on the floor.

25-32   Repeat 2 times, counts 21-24.

33	Lift the right leg up – straight – and with both hips down on the floor.
34	Lower the right leg.
35-36	Reverse counts 33-34.
37-60	Repeat 6 times, counts 33-36.
61-68	Curl up and sit on your feet, with your head on your knees, or as close to the knees as possible, and the hands on the top of your head.
69	Pulse and twist the upper torso to place the right elbow on the left knee.
70	Pulse in center position, head to knees.

71	Twist the upper torso to the other side and pulse and place the left elbow on the right knee.
72	Pulse the upper torso and head down, centered over the knees.
73-84	Repeat 3 times, counts 69-72.
85-168	Repeat counts 1-84.

Be sure that the legs are really straight on counts 1-20 and 33-60, and that the hips are down on the floor. If you find that you are holding your breath on the first 16 counts, which are the most difficult, concentrate on breathing correctly. You'll find that you can then do the exercise quite as well, breathe correctly, and accumulate less tension. Of course, you could also give yourself reminders out loud: "pull in that tummy," or "relax your back." You should be able to talk while exercising, if you are breathing correctly.

FITNESS MINUTES: If your feet get sore from the kneeling section of the exercise – some feet don't like that pressure on them – try placing the balls of the feet on the floor; if your feet or knees are still sore, place something soft on the floor: a towel, your leg warmers, a sweater, etc. This may help. You'll probably find that as your feet develop a better arch and have a slightly different shape – which may take awhile – you'll be comfortable in the original position used in this exercise.

FITNESS MINUTES: Pregnant women should be sure to check with their doctor about doing exercises. Most of them will probably be able to do many of the exercises standing, sitting, lying on the side, or on the back, but absolutely not those performed while lying down on the abdomen.

NUTRITION HINT: The Food and Drug Administration advises pregnant women and nursing mothers not to eat canned tuna more than once a week because of the high levels of mercury in tuna.

****

No. 9-3 – HINGE, PRESS, STAND

Start with 2 knees on the floor and the arms either overhead or in front.

1-4	Hinge back from the knees, keeping the torso in a straight line. The knees should be visible at all times. Pull up the abdomen, and also pull the thighs and hips in toward your center.
5-8	Return to starting position.
9-12	Place the right foot a good distance in front on the floor, knee bent, arms forward, and lean the straight torso forward over the bent right leg to stretch the legs. Arms are extended forward; thighs, hips, and abdomen pull up with a long spine.
13-16	Place the right knee on the floor again.
17-32	Reverse counts 1-16.
33-64	Repeat counts 1-32.
65-68	Place the right foot on the floor in front and stand up.
69-70	Place the right foot back on the floor and kneel.
71-72	Place the left knee on the floor next to the right one.
73-144	Reverse counts 1-72.

FITNESS MINUTES: A good workout should include warm-ups, body conditioning such as isolations, and exercises for stretching and toning up; then aerobic movements such as a repetition, at a good pace, of previously learned steps or a dance-like routine done in a more energetic fashion, if possible – with jumps; then a cooling-down period – a slowing-down time as you repeat movements you've learned. For a longer exercise session, do the whole chapter twice, with a short 5-minute walk in between, or 5 minutes of light running in place, or 5 minutes of knee raises in front with hand weights and arm pulses, and occasionally try these very slowly for greater strength training. For a shorter session, break this all up into small segments to be done throughout the day and even get the long routine done in pieces by the end of day, if that suits you. It is good to vary not only your exercises but also the order in which you do them; otherwise your body will get used to them, do them more efficiently and feel less challenged, and use up fewer calories.

NUTRITION HINT: Many people find that having a pedometer is an added incentive to doing additional movement. Children and seniors might enjoy this also. There's a certain pleasure obtained from aiming at a goal of so many steps and achieving it. Make it a family project – who can add 200 steps each day for so many days in a row, or for two weeks, then someone else in the family gets to try. Or everyone in the family gets a pedometer for the summer holidays. The inexpensive ones seem to work well, without getting involved in calories, just in steps. Make it a rule that ice cream or a candy bar means an extra amount of steps, say 500 more per day for that particular week, so the message is understood that energy in has to be compensated for by energy out.

****

No. 9-4 – TWIST AND SLIM

Stand with the feet slightly apart and parallel; the heels are just a bit off the floor; hands are in pussycat paw position – elbows bent at the sides and close to the body, with the hands in front, hanging down from the wrists.

1	The lower torso – hips and legs – twist toward the right; the heels are slightly off the floor; weight is on the balls of the feet. The shoulders, arms and upper torso remain where they were – facing the front.
2	Reverse count 1. The upper torso and arms remain facing front while the lower torso – hips, legs and feet – face toward the left side.
3-8	Repeat 3 times, counts 1-2.
9+10	Same twisting motion as before, but in threes – to the right, left, right and pause. For a twist walk, place those twisting steps a bit forward, or backward.
11+12	Again in threes – twist – to the left, right, left and pause.
13-16	Repeat counts 9-12. Remember to keep the hands, arms and upper torso as motionless as possible and facing the front as the lower torso twists.
17-32	Repeat counts 1-16 with flat palms facing down at the sides.
33-40	Relax.
41-80	Repeat counts 1-40.

While doing this step be sure that both feet and knees are parallel and twist to the side at the same time.

A small jump on two feet can be added while doing the twisting movement with the lower torso and limbs, as you become more experienced.

FITNESS MINUTES: This is an excellent exercise for stressing forward weight placement. The alignment should always be on a forward diagonal from the heels to the top of the head. The heels should be able to come off the floor easily; the toes should not. (The only time when this is not good alignment is when walking on icy snow. Then, flat feet on the ground, slightly bent knees are best, no pushing off the floor with the ball of the foot, but just lift and step on a flat foot with the body weight centered over it.)

NUTRITION HINT: The Mediterranean way of eating – prevalent in Greece – is said to be a very healthy one. It includes garlic, beans, many fresh vegetables and fruits (rich in antioxidants, fiber, minerals, and vitamins), whole grains (full of fiber, vitamins and minerals not found in refined carbohydrates), and fish (with omega-3 fatty acids that help prevent heart attacks). It is low in meat (with saturated fats that clog up the arteries), and is low in trans fats and empty sugar calories. The fat consumed in the Mediterranean diet is mainly olive oil, a monounsaturated fat, and fats from nuts and seeds. The cheese that is eaten is the lower fat variety like feta and Parmesan; it is eaten daily but in small quantities. A glass of wine often accompanies the meal. Walking and physical activity are a part of everyday life for many.

****

No. 9-5 – SHRUG IT OFF

Stand and face the front left corner – DSL, downstage left is what it's called – with the weight on the bent left leg and the right leg pointed side-back on the floor. The arms are out to the sides, with the palms facing out, but relaxed, not tense, and the elbows slightly bent down.

1	The right shoulder goes forward sharply.
+	The right shoulder goes back to place.
2-4	Repeat 3 times, count 1.

5-8	Place the weight on the bent right leg, with the left leg pointing side-back on the floor, and reverse counts 1-4 with the left shoulder.
9-16	Repeat counts 1-8.
17-32	Reverse counts 1-16 and move the shoulder first to the back then to center.
33-40	Relax.
41-80	Repeat counts 1-40.

FITNESS MINUTES: If you wish to energize this further, add a step to the down stage left corner, on the left foot, on count 1, as the right shoulder goes forward, then 3 times do ball change on counts +2+3+4: a quick step back with the right foot and a step front, in place with the left foot as the shoulder goes forward. Pause for counts 5-8. Reverse for counts 9-16 as you change directions to face the downstage right corner. Later try it without the pause.

NUTRITION HINT: Fresh salmon has become a staple in many people's diets. However, the Environmental Defense, a national environmental group, does not recommend the consumption of farm-raised salmon more than once a month, even though it is less expensive and is available all year. Pregnant women should not consume it at all. The Federal Department of Agriculture, on the other hand, disagrees with them about the amount of PCBs found in farmed salmon and does not limit the quantity to be eaten, provided the skin and the fat just beneath the skin are removed; this is the area containing the bulk of the pollutants and PCBs – polychlorinated biphenyls – cancer causing contaminants.

Wild salmon, however, are predators, have a much lower amount of contaminants than farm salmon, are seasonal, more expensive, have less fat and it is all omega-3 fatty acids. Wild salmon are called either "from Alaska", pink, Coho, or sockeye. Canned salmon is very often wild and is low in mercury compared to tuna fish. Other recommended wild fish are: herring, Atlantic mackerel, tilapia, anchovies, halibut, sea bass, sole, whitefish and sardines, as well as seafood such as mussels and crawfish. If you eat fish several times a week, which you should, try to vary and eat a different kind each time.

****

DANCE ROUTINE – LOCOMOTOR EXPRESS

Turn on the radio. Try the routine with whatever you find just to walk through it once. Then think of some music you have which might be more suitable. How about considering something from the musical "Starlight Express," or even some children's music for a change – "The People on the Bus" or "Puff the Magic Dragon."

1+2	Step diagonally forward on the right foot; then step in back, on the left foot and forward again on the right foot. At the same time the left arm extends out to the side and does 2 shoulder shrugs. We'll make believe these are the wheels warming up for the locomotion.
3-4	Reverse counts 1-2.
5-8	Repeat counts 1-2.
9-16	Do stride jumps in a front-back direction – one foot in front and one in back – with one arm coming forward in opposition to the front leg. Do these 8 times.
17-32	Repeat counts 1-16.
33-64	Do 32 running steps forward in a large circle. The train is in motion. Bring the arms in front with the elbows shoulder high and bent, and the palms higher above and facing you. After 4 running steps bring the arms out to the sides with the palms remaining up and the elbows shoulder high. These are the train windows opening and closing for the 32 counts of running steps.
65-96	Now repeat the step-close-step of counts 1-32. At the same time reach up with first the right then the left arm as though holding onto the strap above for balance.
97-128	Do 32 counts of stride jumps sideways, opening and closing the feet together, or 2 jumps in each position. Meanwhile, open and shut the doors. Cross the forearms in front of you, shoulder high, or down low, with the palms facing down; then press the elbows back to open the doors.
129-136	Do 8 twist walks forward; these are the windshield wipers. Arms are down at the sides with the palms facing down or back.
137-144	Now do 8 twist jumps.
145-160	Repeat the 8 twist walks and 8 twist jumps.

161   Repeat the routine for 4 minutes from the beginning: the wheels, the windows, holding onto the straps, the doors, and the windshield wipers. Have a good trip. Exaggerate the movements.

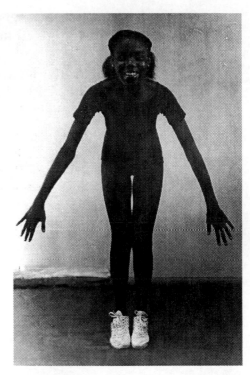

FITNESS MINUTES: An ideal movement program should have variety: weight training for strength and stamina, core conditioning for balance and good posture, aerobic exercise for cardiovascular fitness and stretching for flexibility. Working out in different forms of training, say three each week, insures that you won't get bored while building up added stamina and skills.

NUTRITION HINT: Stay away from quick crash diets. They are very rough on your body. Stick to much of your usual food, if you wish, but eat less. Don't eat empty calories without nutritional value. No sugar; no bad fats; less salt is a good rule. Losing weight this way will take longer than a crash diet but it will be less stressful on your body and will be worth the discipline – it will become a part of your way of caring for yourself. (And to gain weight, eat more.) Basically it's all a question of calories; the more of them you take in without using them up in activity, the more fat you'll have on your body. So if you like the way you are now, continue eating about the same and just think better nutrition. If you weigh too much, eat fewer calories; if you don't weigh enough eat more calories.

****

SUGGESTED READING

American Heart Association. *The American Heart Association Quick and Easy Cookbook: More Than 200 Healthful Recipes You Can Make In Minutes.* NY: Crown Publishing Group, 2001.

Franks, B. Don, Ph.D., Edward T. Howley, Ph.D. and Yuruk Iyriboz, M.D. *The Health Fitness Handbook.* Champaign, Illinois: Human Kinetics, 1999.

Jenkins, Nancy Harmon. *The Mediterranean Diet Cookbook, A Delicious Alternative for Lifelong Health.* NY: Bantam Books, 1994.

Yeager, Selene and the Editors of Prevention. *Prevention's New Foods for Healing.* Emmaus, PA: Rodale Press Inc., distributed by St Martin's Press, 1998.

CHAPTER 10 - JAZZ WALTZ

No. 10-1 – Shoulder Strengthener

No. 10-2 – Rise and Shine

No. 10-3 – Stretch and Relax

No. 10-4 – Shoulder Raise

No. 10-5 – Chassé Side with a Step, Close, Step Turn

Dance Routine – Jazz Waltz

Suggested Reading

No. 10-1 – SHOULDER STRENGTHENER

Start by lying flat on the floor on your abdomen, with the arms straight forward on the floor, elbows as close to the ears as possible.

1-2	Lift both arms up off the floor, a small amount, being sure that the arms are straight, close to the ears, and that the chin and toes remain on the floor.
3-4	Lower the arms to the floor and relax completely.
5-32	Repeat 7 times, counts 1-4.
33-40	Relax; prepare to repeat.
41-80	Repeat counts 1-40.

Some people may be able to lift the arms off the floor just a little bit, with the elbows straight and close to the ears and the chin down; others may not be able to move them at all. So just do the best you can.

FITNESS MINUTES: To get the best results, it is always a good idea to do an exercise as correctly as possible immediately. Just thinking about doing it properly will send the energy in the desired direction so that in this exercise, for example, even though the arms do not seem to move much, eventually the arms will be able to increase their range of movement. This particular exercise is an excellent one for the shoulder area. But doing the exercise incorrectly, with the chin off the floor, every day for a year, will never enable you to do it well. Only accurate practice and an awareness of the desired result can lead to a more exact execution. Thinking about a movement and visualizing how you want to do it are also helpful.

NUTRITION HINT: Some diets prescribe counting calories constantly, which seems like a chore, and you have to make sure that those are nutritious calories. Then there are low carb diets that treat all carbohydrates the same, whereas it is the refined sugars, the empty calories without nutrients, as well as the harmful saturated fats from meats and dairy products that should be drastically reduced. On the other hand, low fat diets allow all foods other than fats to be eaten without restriction. Such diets at least eliminate the bad fats, saturated (meat and some dairy) and trans fats (some dairy and processed foods), but they allow you to eat empty sugar calories with no nutritional value. Sensible diets that include healthy foods in moderate amounts are always best. These diets should have a wide variety of fresh fruits and vegetables, low fat dairy, fish, an occasional serving of low fat meat, whole grains, nuts, and low salt content.

Recent research has found that the leading causes of coronary heart disease are high blood pressure, diabetes, high blood cholesterol and obesity, all of which are diet related, and that antioxidants from fruits and vegetables are a preventive factor. An excessive intake of salt, bad fats, refined sugars, and of all food in general together with an insufficient intake of polyunsaturated fats, omega-3 fats, fiber and water can cause damage to one's health. Whatever changes you plan to make to your diet, keep it nutritious, balanced and enjoyable.

****

No. 10-2 – RISE AND SHINE

Stand with the feet slightly apart and parallel; the arms are out at the sides in jazz hand position, with the forearms about waist high and elbows bent.

1-2   With straight legs, rise up on the balls of both feet. Think of the spine as extending up to the top of the head, which presses up toward the ceiling. The weight should be diagonally forward from the feet to the top of the head. Arms are in starting position.

3-4   With the feet flat on the floor, bend the knees.

5-6   Rise on the ball of the right foot with the leg straight, and the left foot pointed and coming to the side of the standing leg. Bring the right jazz hand in front of the body, with the palm facing but not touching the waist; bring the left jazz hand in back of the body, with the back of the hand facing but not touching the waist.

7-8   Bend the knees, with 2 feet now flat on the floor. The arms remain as in counts 5-6. All of this is excellent for the calves.

9-16   Reverse counts 1-8.

17-32   Repeat counts 1-16.

Practice this step as described; then try it with jumps on 2 legs, then jumps on the right leg, then on the left leg. Try it several times in a row on each leg. Add small kicks to the front or to the side as you jump.

FITNESS MINUTES: When the body is in correct alignment the weight should be forward over the ball of the standing foot and the body on a diagonal line from the foot to the top of the head. As you lift the leg up in front, think of the standing leg as pressing out to the opposite direction – the back – rather than letting it pull forward along with the raised leg, so you will not let the bottom of the hips tuck under – this is what eventually hampers your ease in front extensions, especially if your body tends to be tight. Likewise, if you think of the chest pressing forward, the hips will not be able to remain in an undesirable tucked-under position. So, for many beginners, thinking of chest forward will automatically place the hips into the correct alignment. If you find that you still tend to tuck the hips under during front extensions, try rising up on the ball of the standing foot, just a bit, while keeping that leg very straight but not locked. Hold the weight well forward over the ball of the foot and the body in a forward diagonal from the foot to the head, as you execute the kick to the front. Then lower the standing heel as the raised leg closes down next to the standing foot. Hold onto a barre or a sturdy piece of furniture if necessary. Always start with low kicks; as you practice all the movements in the book, your flexibility and stamina will increase and your extension will slowly become better.

NUTRITION HINT: For anyone attempting to lose weight and keep it off permanently, changing one's eating habits by making the intake of energy (calories) in foods lower than one's output of energy (movement) while getting the most nutritional value out of the food, is essential: Remember portion sizes; ask for a doggy bag; stay away from buffet meals when eating out; or eat and prepare most of your meals at home and then be sure they are low fat, low salt, etc.; don't take seconds; prepare meals and invite friends over; you can converse and eat slowly. Well, what if you did eat too much: don't feel guilty, it's in the past; think about the future – a nice long walk in a museum, park, beach, botanic garden, shopping mall, around your neighborhood – every day for a week, and/or 20 to 50 extra sit-ups and pushups every day for the next seven days, not all at once, but divided into 5 sessions a day. Don't dwell on mistakes or relapses, do something positive; think positive and act positive.

****

No. 10-3 – STRETCH AND RELAX

Stand with the feet slightly apart and parallel and the flat hands on the hips in front.

1-4   Drop the head back and arch the upper torso – the upper ribs and the shoulder area – being careful to keep reaching up toward the ceiling, and not to sink back from the hips. The thighs are pulled up, not turned out; the hips are held in place, with the abdomen and the ribcage pulled up. All the energy goes up, not back.

5-8   Bend forward with a flat back. The hips reach back and the top of the head elongates the spine by reaching frontward. The weight is held as far ahead as possible; you should be able to lift the heels off the floor, but not the toes.

9-12 Drop the head, shoulders and torso forward toward the floor, with the legs still straight. The arms and fingertips relax down toward the floor; but do not try to force the fingers to touch the floor. After you have gone over the workouts in this book a few times you will notice how much closer to the floor your fingers are. If they are on the floor now, try to put your knuckles there; later place the flat palms on the floor, then put the flat palms on the floor in back of the feet.

13-16 Bend the knees and roll up, vertebra by vertebra, till you are standing tall. The head comes up last.

17-64 Repeat 3 times, counts 1-16.

65-72 Relax.

73-144 Repeat counts 1-72.

FITNESS MINUTES: When you use this movement again as a cooling-down exercise after working out or at the end of a class, you should concentrate on doing it fully – you are certainly quite warmed up by then. The flat back should be flatter and the weight more forward than at the beginning of the workout. You also need to be aware of feeling very centered, relaxed, well aligned, and of doing the movement with as little tension as possible. The obvious effort and exertion should have taken place earlier in the class or workout. Now you reap the rewards of your previous work as you stretch more slowly, relax and focus.

NUTRITION HINT: Too much fat in the diet leads to more LDL (bad cholesterol), and less HDL (good cholesterol) and a greater possibility of health problems. A certain amount of cholesterol is needed by the body for the production of brain tissue, digestive juices, some hormones, vitamin D and the bile acids necessary for digesting fat. The body does produce the amount it needs, but an excess supply occurs when people eat too much saturated fat and hydrogenated fat. This excess is the bad cholesterol – LDL, low-density lipoprotein – that accumulates in the arteries, clogs them up and can increase the possibility of heart attacks, strokes and cerebral thrombosis when a clot occurs in a blood vessel in the brain. The good cholesterol – HDL, high-density lipoprotein – absorbs the fat that builds up in the arteries, thus preventing the buildup of cholesterol, and transports it to the liver to be metabolized into bile salts and harmlessly eliminated through the intestines.

****

No. 10-4 – SHOULDER RAISE

Stand with jazz hands extended out at the sides at waist level, elbows slightly bent. Legs are parallel, straight and slightly apart.

1   Raise the shoulders, lifting the whole arm and hand with them. This isolation is easy.

2   Lower the shoulders in place; at the same time, lower the entire right and left arms and jazz hands, as well, to starting position.

3-16   Repeat 7 times, counts 1-2.

17-20   Pause and relax.

21-40   Repeat counts 1-20.

To change this into an isolation exercise just for the shoulders, try not to move the hands from their spot in space. This takes more concentration. To get the correct sensation in your body, press your palms against a piece of furniture or against the wall. You might want to try it sitting cross-legged on the floor, with your hands against the wall. Then try it again without actually pressing against anything, but just thinking about it.

For a more aerobic movement, try this exercise with a loose easy run around the room, as you move the shoulders up and down. Do it with relaxed hands at your sides, and then with jazz hands as in the original exercise. Alternate from one to the other for 8 counts of each.

FITNESS MINUTES: To relax the muscles during a lengthy plane or car ride, do the following: Bring your shoulders up, down, then back and front. Squeeze, hold a few seconds, and relax. Also squeeze together the shoulder blades, the buttocks or the abdomen for a few seconds and relax. Another exercise is to raise the heels then lower them; raise your toes and lower them. Press your abdomen and belly button in toward the back of the chair; hold a few seconds then relax. Lift two bent arms overhead and try to touch your shoulder blades with your hands. Take a big breath and lift the arms overhead; repeat. Relax. Repeat. Be sure to walk around once every hour on a long plane ride. Do the same when driving; stop the car in a safe place and walk a bit once every hour. It will prevent blot clots in the legs.

NUTRITION HINT: Smaller meals, and perhaps more often – four or five instead of three and with smaller portions – are often recommended for losing weight, for better digestion, for less heartburn, and as a preventive measure if you are always ravenously hungry by mealtime and want to consume everything in sight. Those of you who plan to add one or two snacks to your food intake, between your 3 small meals, will find that you won't have to worry about inadvertently increasing your calories if you eat a portion of your breakfast, say 1/2 an orange, for a snack; then when you have soup and a sandwich for lunch, only eat 1/2 the sandwich for lunch and 1/2 as a snack with a cup of tea. The snacking keeps your metabolism up, so you don't have a lessening of energy in mid-morning nor in mid-afternoon. Snacks are not recommended between dinner and bedtime, but you may wish to save your fruit dessert from dinner as a snack so your caloric intake will be no greater than it was before you started snacking.

****

No. 10-5 – CHASSÉ SIDE WITH A STEP, CLOSE, STEP; TURN

Stand facing front with the feet slightly apart and parallel and the knees bent; the hands are in jazz hand position, out to the sides, with the forearms about waist high.

1+2   Chassé to the right side – step, close, step to the side – being careful to transfer the body weight, hips and head, over the last step on the right foot.

3   Do one whole turn to the left on the right foot. The left foot comes up next to the side of the right leg. The head spots directly forward, looking at a spot as long as possible, then quickly revolving around to look at it again before the end

of the turn. The right jazz hand will come in front of the waistline and the left jazz hand will go to the back of the waistline during the turn.

4   Finish the turn by bending the knees and placing both feet flat on the floor side by side and the jazz hands out to the sides once more.

5-16   Repeat 3 times, counts 1-4.

17-32   Reverse counts 1-16 – chassé left, raise the right foot, bring the left jazz hand in front and the right one in back.

33-40   Relax.

41-80   Repeat counts 1-40.

The reminder for this combination is: Travel right, turn left; then travel left, turn right.

To energize this movement further, add a small hop before the chassé.

FITNESS MINUTES: Besides helping your balance and preventing dizziness, spotting will add more brilliance to the turns, but none of these will occur immediately, so keep working to improve the spotting along with the turns. Relax through the neck for effortless spotting. The eyes for this type of turn should focus straight ahead and return to focus on that spot as quickly as possible. For 1/4 turns you simply focus on the next direction you'll be facing either as you get there or just before you get there. On whole turns the head remains facing front till the first shoulder gets there, then the head quickly rotates and returns to face front just about when the 2nd shoulder is in front, before the remainder of the body catches up.

NUTRITION HINT: Take a pinch of skin or rather flesh at your side, below the ribs; if it's more than 1/4 inch check the scale, maybe you need to lose weight. If it is more than an inch you really need to consider the difference between your calorie input and expenditure (output). If you are gaining, you are consuming too many calories compared to the quantity you are burning each day. Intake of calories should equal output of energy. Eat smaller portions. Eat less and do more movement and exercise. Read the Fitness Minutes and Nutrition Hints in this book to get more suggestions for healthy nutrition and exercises. At the same time, remember that heredity can play a part in one's tendency to be heavy, so if it runs in your family, try to lose one pound per week on a continuous basis and you'll see and feel a difference slowly.

****

DANCE ROUTINE – JAZZ WALTZ

How about a nice Johann Strauss waltz or "My Favorite Things" from "Sound of Music". Not jazzy? Then consider Dave Brubeck's "It's A Raggy Waltz", played by the Dave Brubeck Quartet.

1-3	Do either 1 or 2 chassés to the right; finish by stepping on the right foot. The arms are in jazz hand position out to the sides.
4-6	Do 3 running steps to the left while making a whole turn. The right jazz hand is in front and the left jazz hand in back of the waist.
7-18	Repeat 2 times, counts 1-6.
19-21	Jump feet apart; at the same time stretch the arms up, as if yawning.
22-24	Jump feet together; at the same time the arms go down at the sides, the torso drooping and head down slightly.
25-48	Reverse counts 1-24.
49-60	Do 12 jumps in place with the legs alternately kicking out to the front. The arms are out to the sides.
61-63	Jump feet apart and stretch the arms up high.
64-66	Jump feet together and slap thighs 2 times.
67-72	Repeat counts 61-66.
73-96	Repeat counts 49-72.
97-292	Repeat this whole routine for approximately 2-4 minutes. Alternate between walking and running through it.

FITNESS MINUTES: If your posture is starting to look bad from carrying heavy groceries, babies, handbags, etc., always on the same side, switch sides. Try to be ambidextrous. Don't always reach for an item on the top shelf with the same arm; try the other one. Use alternate arms when vacuuming, shoveling snow, etc. Also try this simple exercise. Sit with your buttocks both firmly down, your spine reaching up and forward, from your seat, the back of your neck reaching up to the top of your head with the chin relaxed up just a bit and your shoulders held back. Press your palms down on your thighs as you pull the torso up, and your belly button back and up so your abdomen is very firm. Hold this position as you count to 20 or 25 slowly – that should be about 25 seconds. Don't hold your breath. Relax and try it again. If, while holding the position, you get the feeling that maybe your right or left shoulder is not held back or you are tilting slightly to one side, then adjust your position and continue counting to 25. After doing this a few times a day for a week or two you'll feel your natural corset of muscles strengthening, and you'll see the resulting improvement in your posture.

FITNESS MINUTES: Daily movement – walking and exercise – is as important for seniors as for everyone else. Studies published in the *Journal of the American Medical Association* imply that seniors who get regular exercise are less apt to decline mentally. Women who walked just one and a half hours weekly had improved mental ability as shown on standardized tests, compared with those who exercised less. An enjoyable activity is always best. Tai chi is often mentioned for seniors, for balance, improving bones, and strengthening the mind. Ballroom dancing is excellent since it offers an opportunity to socialize. Many believe that arm movements with hand weights are great for reinforcing the muscles, even for seniors. So pick up a bag of beans in each hand and move them. Read some jokes and laugh, for facial exercise.

NUTRITION HINT: If you have children, nephews, nieces, or young friends, try to get them involved in your workout activities and walks. Research has found that children all over the world, and certainly in this county, are actually getting fat from not being active, from sitting too long in front of the television and computer and from eating too much food but not necessarily the correct foods. When excess calories are consumed but not used up they get stored in the body and become fat. Why should a young child have to start life with the disadvantage of excess fat? Smaller portions of food combined with physical activity would certainly help to correct this and prevent future health problems. The most prevalent preventable cause of death today is said to be obesity.

NUTRITION HINT: Since seniors cannot easily absorb and utilize all the vitamins and minerals contained in foods they eat, they often need to take a supplement. The B vitamins, including B-6, B-12, and folic acid, and vitamin C are especially necessary for them, as well as vitamin D if they do not get much sunshine. A healthy diet of fruits, vegetables, fruit juice, proteins from legumes, beans, eggs, fish, poultry, and meat, as well as nuts, grains, and sufficient water will keep seniors hydrated and provide them with the vitamins, minerals, antioxidants and tasty foods they need. However, calcium, magnesium and zinc are sometimes lacking, so a multivitamin/mineral supplement is suggested; The UC Berkeley Wellness Letter, August 2004, suggests the inexpensive store brands, preferably those with the USP label signifying that the product meets the standards of the U.S Pharmacopeia.

****

SUGGESTED READING

Kent, Allegra, with James and Constance Camner. *The Dancer's Body Book*. N.Y. William Morrow, 1984.

Spilner, Maggie, Walking Editor Prevention Magazine. *Prevention's Complete Book of Walking – Everything You Need to Know to Walk Your Way to Better Health*. NY: Rodale, Inc., 2000.

Tribole, Evelyn, M.S., R.D. *More Healthy Homestyle Cooking*. NY: Rodale Press, distributed by St. Martin's Press, 2000.

CHAPTER 11 - POPS 'N' JAZZ

No. 11-1 – Hips and Abdomen

No. 11-2 – Rib Shift

No. 11-3 – Strong Feet

No. 11-4 – Shoulders

No. 11-5 – Shoulder Area, Arms

No. 11-6 – Knee Pops

Dance Routine – Pops 'N' Jazz

Suggested Reading

No. 11-1 – HIPS AND ABDOMEN

Start supine in hook lying position with the arms down at the sides. The feet and knees are lined up from the hips.

1-4   Slowly stretch the front of the thighs by lifting the pelvis as high as possible. Pull in the abdomen.

5-8   Slowly lower the hips as follows: Start from the top of the neck, round the back, pull in the abdomen, and lower the spine, vertebra by vertebra, so that the waistline gets down before the hips; they go down last.

9-10   With the hands behind the head, lift the head, shoulders, elbows and upper torso and pulse the right elbow toward the outside of the left knee. The waistline should remain on the floor. The spine is rounded.

11-12   Pulse the head and elbows toward the center between the knees.

13-14	Reverse counts 9-10, and pulse the left elbow toward the outside of the right knee.
15-16	Pulse the head toward the center as in counts 11-12.
17-20	Lower the upper torso to the floor, straighten the legs with the arms in a wide U overhead. Press the waistline down toward the floor; pull in the abdomen. Do not turn out the legs; reach out from under and lengthen them out toward the flexed feet.
21-22	Lift the head up in front, leaving the arms and shoulders down on the floor; the abdomen pulls up and the legs stretch all the way out to the flexed feet on the floor.
23-24	Place the head down on the floor.
25-26	Lift the chin and stretch the front of the neck while you look back as far as possible. The shoulders and arms remain down on the floor.
27-28	The head returns to a centered position.
29-36	Repeat counts 21-28.
37-40	Bend the knees and relax the spine, hips, shoulders and neck down on the floor. The arms are at the sides.
41-160	Repeat 3 times, counts 1-40.

Counts 1-16 are especially good for the lower back area.

FITNESS MINUTES: Once you have learned all the exercises in this chapter and can do them easily, do them several times one after the other without stopping in between. You should not get out of breath. You should be able to talk while doing them if you are breathing properly and if you have gradually built up your stamina.

NUTRITION HINT: In order not to feel completely deprived of your favorite foods, which unfortunately may not be the best for your weight or nutrition, once a week treat yourself to a small portion of one of them, e.g., a small scoop of real ice cream, or a small serving of French fries, or a small piece of cheesecake, something different each week, but only a small portion. Meanwhile don't forget to eat healthy, nutritious meals every day; stick to nine fruits or vegetables a day, good fats like olive or canola oil and omega-3 fatty acids found in wild salmon and other fish, lean meat, low fat dairy, skinless poultry, and no empty calories. Eat tasty, healthy meals that you enjoy.

****

No. 11-2 – RIB SHIFT

Stand with the hands either at the sides, on the barre, or holding on to a steady piece of furniture. Legs are a good distance apart and straight.

1-2	Shift the weight over to the right leg as you bend the right knee, keeping the back very straight and tall.
3-6	Shift the ribs to the right, left, right and left.
7-8	Return the ribs to a centered position as you straighten the right leg and center your weight.
9-16	Reverse counts 1-8.
17-64	Repeat 3 times, counts 1-16.

FITNESS MINUTES: This ribcage shift is an excellent warm-up exercise for stretching the calves and centering the hips while isolating the ribs; then, when done twice as slowly for the cooling-down segment, this isolation movement will become even more effortless. You may want to practice this exercise while sitting on the edge of a good solid chair or while sitting on the floor, cross-legged, if you've been having trouble keeping the hips centered; be careful not to tilt the head or upper torso. Varying the arm position also makes it easier for some people: try hands on your head or shoulders, palms together overhead, hands on ribs or on your hips. You'll probably discover that one of these positions enables you to do a better rib isolation than the others. It should carry over to all the other positions.

NUTRITION HINT: Eat healthy foods – especially those you enjoy. To lose weight, consume fewer calories. Include several watery low calorie items like carrots, lettuce, radishes, celery, asparagus, leeks, onions, apples, zucchini, red or green peppers, in your stews, salads, or sandwiches. The bulk will make you feel satisfied with fewer calories and these all contain worthwhile antioxidants.

****

No. 11-3 – STRONG FEET

Stand with the feet slightly apart and parallel; jazz hands are out to the sides, or overhead with hands crossed at the wrists if this helps to remind you to pull up and stand straight and tall. Or place the arms in front, with the elbows bent at shoulder level, and the forearms at right angles with the upper arms, fingers reaching up, a good reminder to hold the head up tall, so the eyes can see the palms directly in front of them or just a bit higher.

1 Lift the right foot in front, just a few inches off the floor, with the knee bent and the toes pointing. The ankle is fully stretched. This movement from the floor should be one of pushing the floor away, in order to use the muscles underneath the foot and get the most benefit from this exercise.

+ Return the foot to the floor.

2-4 Repeat 3 times, to the front, with the same foot.

5-8 Repeat 4 times – to the back, so the foot is in back of the body.

9-12 Repeat 4 times, but now the side of the lifted pointed foot is against the side of the standing calf each time you lift the foot.

13-14 Place the foot on the floor next to the other one, with both knees bent.

15-16 Straighten the legs, with 2 feet on the floor.

17-32 Reverse counts 1-16.

33-128 Repeat 3 times, counts 1-32.

To do this more energetically, run in place, first with the foot in back, the usual way, but with fully pointed feet, then with each foot coming up next to the side of the other leg, pointing the toes and stretching the ankles fully. Also do runs in a circle or a figure 8 around the room, or forward and backward, depending on the available space.

You know your foot is touching the side of the other leg, obviously, when you feel it at the side of the standing leg. Sounds simplistic, but it works well for many people. This is an excellent exercise as a preparation for turns with correct foot placement at the side of the leg.

FITNESS MINUTES: To acquire lovely feet with a good arch, always concentrate on stretching the ankle before you think of the toes, so that the arch will develop higher up in the foot. Then add the pointing of the tips of the toes, for an exquisite arch.

NUTRITION HINT: A glass of wine per day (one 5 oz glass for women, two 5 oz glasses for men) has been found to help keep the heart healthy, due to its antioxidants.

However, the American Cancer Society does not recommend that people with cancer or with a family history of cancer either smoke or drink alcohol. Nor is it recommended that people who do not normally drink should begin to drink wine. But eating grapes, or drinking grape juice (not grape drink), is good; their skins contain saponins, a chemical that helps reduce bad cholesterol. Also good is a glass of dark nonalcoholic wine. Grapes, wines, and dark nonalcoholic wines all contain the antioxidants quercetin and resveratrol.

****

No. 11-4 – SHOULDERS

Stand with the feet slightly apart and parallel; the two arms are in front about shoulder height, with the hands hanging down from the wrists.

1	The left shoulder comes forward as the right shoulder goes back.
+	The right shoulder comes forward and the left shoulder goes back.
2-4	Repeat counts 1+. Hands down, relaxed, from the wrists.
5-8	Repeat the movement, twice as fast.

9-16   Repeat counts 1-8, but with the right hand as before and with the left hand at the side of the body, hanging down from the wrist, and elbow bent in back and forearm close to the body. The shoulder movement will be slow for 4 counts, then fast for 4 counts.

17-24   Reverse counts 9-16.

25-30   Relax.

31-60   Reverse counts 1-30.

61-   Repeat counts 1-60.

For more difficulty add a simple jump on 2 feet as you do the shoulder movement.

If your hands and wrists are relaxed, the hands should shake during this movement.

If you find that your hips also shake and you have trouble isolating your shoulders, try this: Bend down from the waist, with legs straight and with the arms hanging down; shake the shoulders as you raise the torso and concentrate on keeping the hips still by pressing down toward the floor with the thighs, calves, and feet. Continue the shoulder shimmy while you roll up and stand tall. This procedure should eventually work well, and only shoulders will shake without the hips shimmying too.

FITNESS MINUTES: An exercise program such as the one given here, when done on a regular basis, is beneficial not only for those who need to lose weight, but also for those who need to gain. It will increase the muscle strength and muscle mass; through the relaxing effect of exercise there will be less wastage of calories in nervous energy, and eventually the calories will be used to better effect. A feeling of well being, fitness, greater stamina, energy and improved sleep will result and these will enable you to eat properly. As you read through the book and try out the various steps, you'll find notes to refresh your memory as to the benefits to be gotten from a workout.

NUTRITION HINT: Proper sleep is important for better motor skills and also for maintaining your proper weight. You can gain weight by not getting sufficient sleep. Your body and muscles get sluggish, you don't have as much energy; you eat more. Your body tries to conserve energy, not use it up, and you gain weight. Also, lack of sleep prevents the level of leptin from rising in the body. Leptin is a hormone that is only produced during sleep. It helps control appetite; the less leptin you have the hungrier you feel. So try to get more sleep if you need to lose weight. Do some simple, effortless, arm or body swings or sways to put you in a relaxed, sleepy mood before bedtime if more strenuous movement wakes you up.

****

No. 11-5 – SHOULDER AREA, ARMS, HANDS

Stand with the arms extended out to the sides, palms down; weight is on the bent left leg, with right foot pointed and extended side-back. Face downstage left – the front left corner.

1-2	The right shoulder circles forward, up, back and down in place, without any extraneous movements.
3-4	Reverse counts 1-2 and circle the left shoulder.
5-8	Repeat counts 1-4.
+	Reach out to the side with the right arm without moving the ribcage: the right shoulder comes slightly forward as the arm reaches out toward the side.
9	The right arm and shoulder return to place.
10	Pause.
+11-12	Repeat counts 9-10.

+13-16	Reverse counts 9-12.
17-24	Repeat counts 1-8, with the weight on the bent right leg and facing downstage right; the left leg points side-back.
25-32	Repeat counts 17-24, but with the palms pressing out to the sides and the hands in a vertical position; do not let the fingers drop down. Think of the entire palm pressing out to the side and the fingers going up and towards you.
33-64	Repeat counts 1-32 but reverse the direction of the shoulder circles and do back, up, forward and down.
65-128	Repeat counts 1-64.

The arms, when extended to the sides with the palms pressing out, in a vertical position, do make a somewhat circular movement along with the shoulders. To prevent a larger circular motion of the arms, think of the palms as remaining pressed against a particular spot in space, or against the wall.

FITNESS MINUTES: Palms pressing out vertically, especially with straight arms, during shoulder circles, is excellent for the arms. If you feel a slight burn through your arms, simply shake them out, relax, and don't do that exercise again until tomorrow.

NUTRITION HINT: When your sweet tooth craves a bit of food, try dried or fresh fruits instead of candy. These will satisfy your desire, and provide great nutrition. Berries are full of antioxidants that assist in absorbing free radicals – toxic molecules produced by the body. Cranberries raise the level of HDL – good cholesterol that absorbs the fat that clogs up the arteries. Blueberries assist in keeping arteries elastic, thus lessening the possibility of heart disease, currently the greatest health risk of American women, and which can be caused by diabetes, high blood pressure and high levels of bad cholesterol – LDL. Figs provide calcium, apricots provide beta-carotene; and they all taste terrific. Fresh fruits have less sugar than dried fruits. The old saying is "an apple a day keeps the doctor away," but other fruits are good too, and fruit skins have lots of minerals and antioxidants.

****

No. 11-6 – KNEE POPS

Stand with feet slightly apart and parallel; arms are out at the sides.

+	Lift both heels.
1	Return the heels to the floor.
2	Pause.

+3-4	Repeat counts +1-2.
+5	Step on the balls of the feet – right, then left – with the feet apart and with both hands reaching up high in front and flicking down from the wrists.
6-8	Slowly lower the heels.
+	Do a knee pop by lifting the heels while bending the knees and without disturbing the torso. The shoulders and head do not move.
9	Return the heels to the floor.
10	Pause.
+11-12	Repeat. This is excellent for the calves.
13-36	Repeat 3 times, counts +5-12.
37-40	Place feet in starting position.
41-80	Repeat counts 1-40.

In knee pops – counts +9-12 – the hips should not move. To be aware of whether or not your hips are motionless, place the right pinky on the front of the right hip, and the left pinky on the front of the left hip, with the palms facing up and elbows out at the sides. The thighs should isolate themselves from the hips, so that the legs can move and the knees bend without disturbing the hips.

FITNESS MINUTES: Knee pops can also be done with the "pop" itself on the strong beat instead of on the offbeat; you've seen this on television. The example given here, however, has the syncopation characteristic of jazz dance, so the pop occurs on the offbeat. Sharp movements accentuated by a pause are often used in jazz dance. Try it both ways.

NUTRITION HINT: Fat-laden diets are bad for the heart and also lead to high blood pressure and diabetes, the chronic ailments of obesity. These fats are the trans fats (hydrogenated oils), found in fried fast food, baked goods such as cookies, and in most margarines and shortening. Also bad are saturated fats from red meat, chicken skin, and dairy products such as cheese and whole milk (the cream at the top). These are solid, or almost solid, at room temperature. All of these raise the amount of bad cholesterol (LDL) in the body, clog the arteries with fat deposits and possibly lower the level of good cholesterol (HDL). Avoid organ meats like liver and kidney that are full of cholesterol; or just consume them occasionally. Eat red meat once or twice a week instead of five times (otherwise remove the fat before cooking); remove the chicken skin; check the labels on dairy products and purchase those with reduced fat content. Many packaged meats and poultry come with "low fat" labels. Even canned broths come with labels telling the buyer that the fat content is low, when that's the case. These do help the purchaser make a wiser choice.

****

DANCE ROUTINE – POPS 'N' JAZZ

"When I Think of You," Janet Jackson; or "I Didn't Mean to Turn You On," Robert Palmer, would be suitable. Look through your collection or listen to the radio and get ready to do this routine.

1-4   Do 4 chugs – a small sliding jump – forward. At the same time, the right arm extends forward, the left hand is on the hip, and the shoulders shimmy forward and backward.

5+6   Jump with the feet apart, sideways, together, and apart again with the arms out at the sides.

7+8   Shift the ribs to the right, left, right, with the feet still apart.

+   Jump and bring the feet together.

9-16+   Reverse counts 1-8+.

17-30   Do 14 slow or 28 fast running steps in place or in some sort of a pattern – a figure 8, a letter of the alphabet, a geometrical figure – if space is available. The arms are out at the sides. The arms pulse in and back at the shoulders on each

116

step. See counts +9-16 of No. 5 in this chapter. On the last running step bring the feet together on the floor.

31   Bring the arms overhead, crossed at the wrists, and straighten the knees.

+32   Do one knee pop.

33-64   Repeat counts 1-32, but do the chugs moving back; then on counts 17-30 press the palms out at the sides and make the accent of the pulse go out to the side.

65   Repeat this entire routine for 2-4 minutes. As in previous routines, walk instead of running, or step out to the side instead of doing stride jumps to start; gradually add the jumps and the running. Slow down again, and so on.

FITNESS MINUTES: If you are keeping up with your exercise schedule, then you deserve to treat yourself to a new pair of sneakers or running shoes. They last only 400 or 500 miles; otherwise get them after going through the whole book one more time. It would be a well-deserved treat for you. For now, how about getting a set of hand weights. They're available in sports supply stores.

NUTRITION HINT: There are good fats – monounsaturated and polyunsaturated – found in canola, flaxseed, corn, olive oil, peanut oil, sunflower oil, some vegetable oils, avocados, as well as in nuts – (unsalted) almonds, cashews and walnuts. They lower the level of bad cholesterol in the body and are essential for the absorption of fat soluble vitamins. While nuts are good for you, they are also a source of energy, and full of calories, so watch how many you eat, or eat less of something else to compensate. Remember, a certain amount of fat (good fat) is essential for the body, especially if you are to profit from the fat soluble vitamins and beta-carotene that you take. Fat is also vital for the growth and development of infants, to maintain healthy hair and skin and to store energy. It is used in several hormonelike components and helps control essential bodily functions and blood pressure. Fat is considered to be so necessary for the absorption of certain vitamins and beta-carotene that food relief organizations dealing with Third World nations on starvation diets include oil along with rice, grains, etc., so people will absorb nutrients more easily. Therefore don't try to eliminate all fat from your diet.

****

SUGGESTED READING

American Heart Association. *The New American Heart Association Cookbook,* 25th Anniversary Edition. NY: Times Books, Random House, 1998.

Shafarman, Steven. *Awareness Heals – The Feldenkrais Method for Dynamic Health.* NY: Perseus Books at HarperCollins Publishers, 1997.

Carper, Jean. *Food –Your Miracle Medicine.* NY: HarperCollins, 1993.

CHAPTER 12 - SYNCHRONIZED LIMBS

No. 12-1 – Abdomen and Torso

No. 12-2 – Side Extension and Relaxation

No. 12-3 – Oppositional Leg Raising

No. 12-4 – Flick and Press

No. 12-5 – Isolation of Body Parts

Dance Routine – Synchronized Limbs

Suggested Reading

No. 12-1 – ABDOMEN AND TORSO

Start supine, flat on your back, with straight legs and pointing toes. Hands are behind your head with the elbows resting on the floor.

1-2	Pull the belly button in and up, and press the waistline down into the floor. At the same time lift the elbows, head, and upper torso off the floor, and flex the feet.
3-4	Return the upper torso, head and elbows down to the floor, and point the toes.
5-8	Repeat counts 1-4.
9-16	Bring the arms forward. Bend the right leg with the foot remaining on the floor, raise the torso, and sit up. The straight leg has a flexed foot.
17-24	Do 8 small pulses forward from the hips, with the arms in front and jazz hands.
25-32	Roll the torso back down to the floor, placing the arms on the floor overhead, hands under your head, and gradually straighten both legs.
33-64	Reverse.
65-128	Repeat counts 1-64, but do only 4 small pulses forward from the hips; place the hands on the floor in back of you for the next 4 counts, as you press the waistline forward, with the chest held high. Then round the torso and roll down to the floor – same as on counts 1-64.
129-	Repeat counts 1-128.

FITNESS MINUTES: Whenever an exercise calls for pulling in the abdomen, be sure to think of pulling the belly button back and up; it makes for a firm, tightly pulled up abdomen. To test this, place one hand on your abdomen and try pulling in the abdomen, first without thinking of the belly button, and then try it with the belly button pulling back and up. You'll get a flat abdomen more quickly by following this suggestion.

NUTRITION HINT: Here's an easy, healthy stir fry recipe for two; double it for four, etc. Take a large skillet, put about 1-2 tablespoons of spray olive oil (or substitute canned low-salt chicken broth or water for this), 1/2 to 3/4 cup each of three different vegetables; any vegetable will do, left over, canned (even beets or asparagus), frozen, or thinly sliced fresh vegetables, an assortment of spices, and if you wish, a tomato, a small amount of green, red, or yellow peppers. If you want to have potatoes or yams (1 medium per person), do not peel white potatoes, the skins are stacked with minerals and vitamins; wash well and slice thinly. If you wish to use proteins, too, add skinless chicken, or turkey, or low fat meat – pork, lean beef, or veal – or fish – scrod, cod, or pollock – cut into small pieces; cook it together with the vegetables. Stir and cook; add a bit of boiling water if necessary; keep stirring; don't let it burn. If you plan to have pasta, or brown or white rice (1/2 cup, before cooking) instead of potatoes, then cook it beforehand and stir it in after the vegetables are cooked. Heat it all a bit longer. Otherwise serve the pasta or rice and place the vegetables, etc. over it. Any leftovers are tomorrow's lunch or part of tomorrow's dinner.

****

No. 12-2 – SIDE EXTENSION AND RELAXATION

Start on your side with both knees slightly bent. One hand is under your head and the other is in front on the floor, to assist you in maintaining your balance.

1	Turn out the top, bent knee, so the knee points up toward the ceiling, with the foot pointing.

2	Lift the knee up toward your shoulder; the toes are still pointing. You should turn out the leg as much as possible, without moving the hips.

3-4	Extend the leg up to the side till it is straight; toes are pointing.
5-7	Flex the foot and lower the straight leg down to the floor. The leg stretches out from under, to the heel of the flexed foot. For a higher extension, relax the leg under the thigh, near the buttocks.
8	Relax the leg and bend it over the other leg.
9-32	Repeat 3 times, counts 1-8.
33-40	Roll over on your back and shake out the legs – quickly flexing and straightening them, either on the floor or up toward the ceiling – excellent for relaxation.
41-48	Roll over to the other side and prepare to reverse the exercise.

49-96   Repeat counts 1-48.

97-192   Repeat counts 1-96.

FITNESS MINUTES: Do not neglect the feet. As a general rule feet are naturally either both strong and sturdy but without a high arch, or are beautifully arched, but weak. Strength and beauty can both be acquired through exercise. The calves and legs have different muscles working when the feet are flexed from the ones at work when they point, so concentrate on using them as described, while doing the leg extensions in this exercise, to get the full benefit of the movement. When you go through the book a second time, you will know the sequence of each exercise more readily and be even better able to concentrate on specific areas, such as the feet, which you may have neglected at first in your enthusiasm to learn each movement.

NUTRITION HINT: Spices add such wonderful flavors to foods that if you are cutting down on salt, as we all should, using spices will make you forget about the lack of salt. *Parsley, Sage, Rosemary and Thyme,* as the Simon and Garfunkel song goes, are delicious in soups and stews and so are other spices. Besides being flavorful, spices have been found by researchers at the Georgetown University Medical Center, the U. S. Department of Agriculture, the National Cancer Institute of India and the University of California, among others, to be strong antioxidants. Spices are healthy for you whereas salt is not. See Glossary.

****

No. 12-3 – OPPOSITIONAL LEG RAISING

Start on your abdomen, in prone position, with the legs straight, close together, and not turned out. The arms are straight on the floor, alongside the ears.

1-2   Raise the straight right arm up off the floor without moving the shoulders, so that they remain even and one is not higher than the other. At the same time lift the straight left leg up off the floor in back, just a few inches. The hips remain on the floor.

3-4   Lower the right arm and the left leg to the floor.

5-8   Reverse counts 1-4. This is an excellent exercise for the buttocks.

9-32	Repeat 3 times, counts 1-8.
33-40	Relax.
41-120	Repeat 2 times, counts 1-40.

It is best to do small movements of the arms and legs and to do them correctly, being sure that the shoulders and hips are even. Hips remain on the floor. Slowly and gradually try to increase the range of movement. However, there should be no side-to-side movement in the shoulder or hip area.

FITNESS MINUTES: If you hold your breath while exercising, make a point of consciously inhaling and exhaling – slowly or very slowly, depending on the exercise – at definite movements or counts in the sequence. The inhalation and exhalation must be continuous and take the same amount of time as the movement or counts. The general rule is: Inhale when you stretch, expand, or are in a released position – there is more space inside you for air. Exhale when the body is contracted, curled up – there is less space inside you for air, and you are better and more easily able to concentrate on pulling up and tightening the abdominal muscles. However, occasionally, you may want to try doing the reverse of this just to see how that suits you.

NUTRITION HINT: A cup of hot chocolate is excellent for you. (The dark chocolate is best.) Heating chocolate releases more of the flavonoids in it – they can raise the level of good cholesterol (HDL) – and they act as antioxidants, and help prevent damage to cells. Research has found that dark chocolate even helps to lower blood pressure. You can also eat a morsel of dark chocolate, not just drink it, but do watch the calories and only eat a small piece.

****

No. 12-4 – FLICK AND PRESS

Stand with the left palm flat on the side of the left hip and the other hand down at the side. Face the front left corner – downstage left – with the feet slightly apart and parallel and with the left heel off the floor and the left knee bent.

1-2	Flick the right hand up overhead, with the fingers hanging down in front with a long finger line, high wrist and a straight arm; no knuckles should appear in the right hand. The left wrist remains at the hip. At the same time the torso leans back slightly from the hips.
3-4	Lower the straight arm down in front. The wrist leads the movement, so that the fingers are highest and the

123

palm faces forward, flat. Continue the movement of the arm to the back, the palm facing down and flat, with the fingers long. The torso now leans forward slightly from the hips. The left heel is on the floor; the right heel comes off the floor and the right knee bends.

5   The right hand flexes in the opposite direction, with the fingers pointing toward the back; the right shoulder presses forward slightly; the left hand comes in front, with the elbow bent down and the hand flexed back at the wrist so that the fingers point toward the left wall.

6   The left hand now goes slightly in back of the body – at the side – with the elbow bent up and the left shoulder forward; the wrist is flexed so that the fingers point toward the back of the room and the palm faces up. The right hand goes in front at the side, with the elbow bent down and the hand flexed back at the wrist; the fingers point toward the right wall, and the palm faces forward. The hands are doing the reverse of count 5

7   Same as count 5.

8   Hold the position from count 7.

9-12   Relax. Place the right wrist on the side of the right hip.

13-24   Reverse counts 1-12.

25-96   Repeat 3 times, counts 1-24.

97-   Try it without the pause of counts 9-12, and do it 8 times. Remember that the next heel comes up on the 5th count of each repetition.

For lack of a better name, I'm calling the sequence on counts 1-4 a False Samba, because it is not really a samba, but it has the swaying movement of the torso leaning forward and backward that is associated with the samba. The samba can also sway with a side-to-side torso movement, but not in this version.

FITNESS MINUTES: Practice and energize the arm movements given in any step description further by using them with simple hops, runs, prances, side jumps, stride jumps, and large runs, for variety. This is also excellent for better coordination and for use of all body areas. For strengthening the arms, the addition of weights is a bonus, especially when you work out very slowly and smoothly. If you do not own any hand weights, consider using containers with handles, such as medium or large size laundry detergent bottles; these are heavy so do one arm at a time or use a smaller dish detergent that is easy to hold. You might like to know that muscle weighs more than fat, but it takes less space in your body, so if you start to feel firm and trim and find you weigh more, that's why. Exercising with weights builds strong bones and muscles, which is good because muscles store carbohydrates, and this causes the body to keep the blood sugar lower and to burn fat.

FITNESS MINUTES: It is important to consider arms and hands when learning a movement sequence. Careful practice of these should keep them strong, supple and expressive. The use of the hands as an extension of the arms gives character and personality to an action; notice how some great dancers or actors use theirs. We can all think of someone we've seen on television who repeatedly uses just one hand movement till we become more aware of this than of the message in the speech.

NUTRITION HINT: An important aspect of healthy eating is to know when you should push the plate away from you, get up and maybe go for a walk instead of eating more.

****

No. 12-5 – ISOLATION OF BODY PARTS

Stand with the feet parallel and the legs straight. The elbows are bent out to the sides, with flat palms on the hips at the sides; fingers point down.

1-8   The ribcage shifts side 8 times, to the right, left, etc., one movement per count. See Chapter 11 for shifts. Press the heels down into the floor as you pull up the legs and thighs to help prevent the development of heavy thighs. Keep the shoulder height the same throughout.

9-12   The arms reach straight down, out to the sides and overhead with the palms facing out. The heels of the palms press out and the fingers press up from the wrist, so the line from fingertip to wrist is very long. When the arms get overhead, place the right hand over the left palm, with both palms facing directly up, not diagonally forward.

13-20   Shift the head forward and back – one movement per count. Keep the chin line level throughout; the head should move directly forward and back without involving the shoulders at all.

21-22   The arms go down through the sides and then bend as the elbows go out at the sides and the pinky of each hand goes on the ribs in front.

23-24   Repeat the movement of counts 9-12 but do it quickly in one count and then repeat the arm movement of counts 21-22 and do this in one count; bend the knees as the hands go to the ribs.

25-26   Do a double hip lift to the right: the hips go to the right, return halfway to center, go to the right again then return to center; the knees are still bent and the hands are on the ribs, as before.

27-28   Reverse counts 25-26 to the left.

29   Open the right hand out in a jazz hand, with fingers stretched wide apart and palm facing forward, without moving the elbow.

30   Open the left hand out in a jazz hand, as in count 29.

31   Lift the shoulders up while keeping the hands in their same spot in space; this will cause the arms to extend and straighten a bit to the sides.

32   Bend the elbows a bit; lower the shoulders to a centered position; place the forearms parallel to the floor at about waist-high position, with jazz hands.

33-34   Without moving the hands from their exact spot in space, circle the right shoulder forward, up, and down in back. The elbow will straighten slightly as the shoulder is lifted and then it will bend as the shoulder returns to place, in order not to move the hand from its spot. Try not to relax the hands; maintain the stretched jazz hand position.

35-36   Reverse counts 33-34 with the left shoulder.

37-40   Same as in counts 33-36, but now do shoulder circles with both shoulders together and do this two times.

41-42   Rise up on the balls of the feet, with straight legs and with the thighs pulled up. At the same time return the hands to their original position – flat palms at the sides of the hips, with the fingers pointing down.

43-44	Lower the heels to the floor; continue pulling the legs up; the weight is on a slight diagonal forward from the heels to the top of the head. The top of the head presses up toward the ceiling while keeping the chin level – neither raised nor lowered.
45-46	Bend the knees with the same good alignment as before.
47-48	Straighten the legs.
49-64	Repeat 2 times, counts 41-48, an excellent movement for the calves.
65-128	Reverse counts 1-64.
129-	Repeat counts 1-128.

Practice the double hip lifts of counts 25-28 separately till you do them smoothly.

Practice the head pecks while walking, like pigeons do.

To add jumps, try the following: Counts 1-8, do small jumps with the feet together while doing rib shifts to the side. Counts 9-22, do prances with the knees coming high up in front. Counts 23-24, do jumps in place with the feet together. Counts 25-28, no jumps, just do hip lifts. Counts 29-64, do small, plain jumps on 2 feet, or with the feet shooting out to the side together – 2 times to the right, then 2 times to the left.

FITNESS MINUTES: The University of Vermont, the University of Beijing and a Korean and Hong Kong study found that Tai chi, a gentle martial art, is an excellent exercise, greatly improving balance on one leg, strengthening thigh muscles due to all the bent knee positions, and increasing bone density. All these help to prevent falls with the risk of fractures, so practicing Tai chi is especially rewarding for seniors. They can find videos in libraries and stores, and classes in health clubs, Y's and Adult Education programs at colleges and community centers. This would be an excellent cross-training activity for many; other beneficial activities for seniors are walking, weight lifting for strength while using light hand weights, water exercises with supervision at a swimming pool, ballroom dancing for socializing, and exercises for flexibility, stamina, coordination and strength. It's important for seniors to continue to have activity daily once they retire.

NUTRITION HINT: Vitamin D – the sunlight vitamin – prevalent in fiber-rich foods, mackerel, salmon, and fortified milk, has been found by British researchers to also help prevent fractures in elderly people. Fifteen minutes of sun, outdoors, is recommended daily as being very beneficial for absorbing vitamin D.

****

DANCE ROUTINE – SYNCHRONIZED LIMBS

Put on some music – anything you wish. Be sure you know all the movements from No. 5 – Isolation of Body Parts; we'll now do them with synchronized limbs.

1-8   Do 4 rib shifts as you step out to the side and in place with first the right foot, then the left, the right and the left.

9-12   Do stride jumps sideways, 2 times, as the palms go out to the sides and overhead.

13-20   Run in place as you do head pecks forward and back.

21-24   Continue running in place as the pinkies go to the ribs.

25-28   Knees bend as you do hip lifts to the right and to the left.

29-30   As the jazz hands go out to the sides, jump 2 times with feet apart.

31-32   While the shoulders go up and down, jump 2 times with the feet together.

33-40   Do stride jumps 4 times – feet apart and together – as you do the shoulder circles.

41-48   Rise up on the balls of the feet and hold the position for 6 counts; then bend the knees for 2 counts.

49-50   Run in place as you flick both hands high overhead in front.

51-52   Run in place 2 times as you press both palms down and back at the sides.

53-64   Repeat 3 times, counts 49-52.

65-   Repeat the entire routine from the beginning and continue doing it for 4 minutes of non-stop movement.

FITNESS MINUTES: Researchers at the University of Illinois at Urbana-Champaign recommend using bleach and water to kill bacteria in the home and other places. Rubbing alcohol is also handy to use; rinse with water. Using antibiotic cleaning agents is not recommended because this leads to the formation of strains of bacteria that will be resistant to antibiotics and impossible to control; so when you clean the kitchen and elsewhere, remember to use bleach and water, not antibiotic cleaners. Rather than using an antibiotic soap to wash your hands, use plain soap and water.

FITNESS MINUTES: A reminder for those of you who are interested mostly in the aerobic aspect of exercise: All continuous movement and exercise is aerobic – some more strenuously so than others. Nevertheless, a well-rounded movement program should include exercises to strengthen and stretch the muscles as well as to condition the cardiovascular system. Other important aspects of exercise that the person practicing at home should think about are: awareness of tension, relaxation, alignment, and centering of the body. The Cooper Institute in Dallas believes that a balanced program can improve your bone density while lowering your blood pressure and cholesterol levels and is more important for fitness than just losing weight would be. They recommend that newcomers do as much as possible, even just 10 minutes a day, 3 days per week, and gradually build the duration up to 1 hour each day, which is ideal.

NUTRITION HINT: Scientists at the Mayo Clinic have found that diabetics who are middle aged or older are better off when they do their exercise on a regular basis rather than sporadically. They recommend brisk walking five days a week, gradually building up the amount to 40 minutes per day. Walking is easily accessible to the majority. It is excellent for those with high cholesterol, obesity problems, and high blood pressure and can be done in conjunction with an exercise program such as the one in this book. It can also be combined with an agreeable outing to the park, zoo, botanical garden, museum, beach, boardwalk, a walk to the library, etc.

****

SUGGESTED READING

Hensrud, Donald, Jennifer Nelson, Cheryl Farberg and Maureen Callahan. *The New Mayo Clinic Cookbook, Eating Well for Better Health*. Menlo Park, Calif.: Oxmoor House, 2004.

Hughes, Russell Meriweather. *The Gesture Language of the Hindu Dance / La Meri*. NY: Arno Press, 1979.

Maisel, Edward. *Tai Chi for Health*. NY: Barnes and Noble, Inc., 1999.

Vaganova, Agrippina. *Fundamentals of the Class Dance*. NY: Dover, 1971.

CHAPTER 13 - CREATIVE MIX

No. 13-1 – BUTTOCKS AND THIGHS

Start in a prone position – on your abdomen – with your hands on your back to become aware of your hips remaining on the floor and of the lower back staying relaxed.

1-4   Leave the hips on the floor as you tighten the buttocks. Then bend the knees and lift the feet up in back just a little bit. The hips remain on the floor.

5-6   Lift the right knee off the floor, with both hips on the floor.

7-8   Return the right knee to the floor, leg still bent.

9-12   Reverse counts 5-8.

13-20   Repeat counts 5-12.

21-24   Straighten the legs and shake the hips out by rolling slightly to the right and left sides.

25-96   Repeat 3 times, counts 1-24.

FITNESS MINUTES: For you who have done the plain version of the steps in the book and will soon wish to go back and energize them, here is a hint: The way to energize any of the warm-up exercises is first to learn them very well and slowly, then to increase the speed at which you do them while performing them just as accurately. Do one exercise after the other at a good pace for 10 to 15 minutes, without stopping, but repeating the series as often as necessary for that length of time; do this only after you know the movements well. Return to the slower speed now and then to check for accuracy, to gain the strength obtained from doing them at a slower tempo, or because you want to concentrate on relaxing certain muscle areas while working other muscles, e.g., relaxing the lower back while concentrating on pulling up the abdomen. To cool down before finishing your workout, also proceed slowly.

NUTRITION HINT: Remember to watch your serving sizes if you have problems with too much cholesterol. A three-ounce portion of meat that does not contain much fat, such as pork tenderloin, beef round or veal, is best. If you see a lot of fat in a piece of meat at the store, either do not buy it or remove the fat before cooking it. Turkey or chicken breasts are always good protein choices, but you should remove the fat and skin from any turkey and chicken. Eggs are also an excellent protein choice; four per week is considered right for most people and even one per day is all right for some; eggs have a high cholesterol content, but they have excellent nutrients such as choline that make up for this and they are easily absorbed by the body, so they are a good choice of protein. However, people with very high levels of cholesterol would probably do best having just one a week or none. A portion of cheese is about your thumb size, but eat the low fat variety; portion size for grain is 1 ounce (1 slice of whole wheat bread, 1/2 whole wheat English muffin, or 1/2 to 1 cup of ready-to-eat breakfast cereals);

portion size for whole wheat pasta, spaghetti, brown rice, or polenta is 1/2 cup cooked; and for French fries, it seems, it is ten fries though none might be better.

****

No. 13-2 – HIP LIFTS

Stand with the feet slightly apart and parallel. Arms are extended out at the sides with the palms facing down

1	Lift the hips up to the right side. At the same time look down at the space between the feet. Be aware of your shoulders; you can see them with your peripheral vision as you look down. The shoulders must not move during this hip isolation. The legs are both straight.
2	Return the hips to center.
3	Lift the hips up to the left, while looking down and being very aware of the lack of movement in the shoulder area.
4	Return the hips to center.
5-32	Repeat 7 times, counts 1-4.
33-36	Bend the knees and place the hands in jazz hand position out at the sides with the forearms parallel to the floor and the elbows slightly bent.
37-68	Repeat the hip lift movement – to the right, center, left, and center – as before, but with the knees bent and the eyes forward.
69-136	Repeat counts 1-68.

For sharper and more syncopated hip movements, start at the very last second, and then quickly lift the hip to the side. When you have very little time for exercise, get double the value out of 5 minutes by adding hand weights to the arm movements or jumps. If you don't own weights, start with something that's not breakable – a can of fruit, or a bag of beans or a bottle of laundry detergent that has a handle – until you get weights. In this exercise, for example, you could have the palms facing up and pulse the right hand toward your shoulder and the left one down, 2 times for each hip lift, then reverse the arms as you reverse the hips, and do it slowly, or try one arm at a time.

FITNESS MINUTES: For better muscle balance in your daily life, try to become aware of how you do what you do physically. Do you carry packages on either arm, or on the left, in order to have the right one available? Do you carry your little child on either hip? Depending on the distance, front or back is better. When standing or bending to pick an object, is your weight centered over both legs? Do you vary and put your balance on either the right or the left, or always on the same one? Do you reach for the top shelf with either hand? Which shoulder carries your shoulder bag or on what side is your wallet? Which arm does the sweeping, vacuuming or snow removal, and then on which leg is your weight? Everyone has a preference for using a specific arm or leg, and it takes concentration and effort to vary this, especially when one is under pressure to finish a task. But the use of variety, where feasible, is a good idea.

NUTRITION HINT: Instead of using a rich tartar sauce for fish, or a rich salad dressing, you'll find that one made with plain low fat yogurt is excellent. Drain the liquid out of it overnight; and add any ingredients you wish – pickles, garlic, onions, scallions, spices, relish or mustard. Experiment. It makes a delicious and healthy dressing; but don't use too many salty items.

****

No. 13-3 – INSTEP STRENGTHENER

Stand with the feet slightly apart and parallel. The wrists are crossed overhead, with jazz hands facing forward.

1	Extend the right leg forward, brushing forward so the toes of the foot remain on the floor, with the heel off the floor, the ankle extended and the legs straight.
+	Press the ball of the right foot into the floor in front, with the extended leg straight.
2	Lift the pointing foot off the floor as the ball of the foot pushes off the floor, strongly stretched and pointing down to the toenail. Both legs are held straight. This is important; without adequate stretches with straight, pulled-up leg muscles, the thighs and hips could develop into bulgy, rather than long muscles.
+3+4	Repeat 2 times, counts +2.
5-6	Close the right foot to the left one; bend knees.
7-8	Straighten both legs.
9-16	Reverse. This, and the version described below, is excellent for the calves.
17-128	Repeat 3 times, counts 1-16; repeat counts 1-64.

For variety, this exercise can also be done with the standing leg bent. The torso is still pulled up. The knees should be over the feet. The weight is held forward and the body pulls up to the top of the head. On counts 5-6, instead of bending both knees, do the opposite and straighten both knees. Then bend the knees on counts 7-8 before reversing the exercise.

FITNESS MINUTES: The hands are crossed overhead to serve as a reminder to pull up the torso. The bellybutton is pulled up and back; the bottom of the breastbone is likewise pulled up and back, making for a long straight upper torso as the back of the ears, neck and the top of the head reach up. To top it off, lift the shoulders and drop them down in back. With practice you can even relax and have the position feel absolutely effortless.

NUTRITION HINT: The salads at all the fast food places, as well as at museums, are just great for those watching their calorie intake. But use a minimum of dressings; they are full of calories and salt; they're very tasty and a little bit goes a long way. The oil and vinegar dressings seem to be available at all places, upon request; they have far fewer calories.

****

No. 13-4 – HIP LIFT WITH OFFBEAT HAND

Stand with the feet slightly apart and parallel; the hands hang down from the wrists like puppydog or pussycat paws, and are held out in front with the forearms close to the body, elbows bent and in back.

1	Lift the right hip up to the right.
+	On the offbeat, the right hip returns to the center. At the same time the right hand opens into a wide, stretched jazz hand position, with the fingers pointing down toward the hip, the palm facing the back, and the remainder of the arm in starting position.
2-8	Repeat 7 times, counts 1+. Relax the hand into puppydog paw position on the beat, as you do the hip lift.
9-12	Pause.
13-20	Reverse count 1-12.
21-80	Repeat 3 times counts 1-20.

If this step is too difficult, try crossing your wrists in front and just concentrate on doing the hip movements without using any arms, till you feel more secure; then add the arms.

Vary this with a jump in place then a hip lift to the side, as you land. Or, as you jump, extend the feet and legs a bit out to one side; then land and do the hip lift to the other side.

FITNESS MINUTES: No time to practice. Think positive. Do a small portion of your workout first thing in the morning, before eating. It's energizing, a great way to start the day and you'll feel good about yourself for having done this. After breakfast take a ten-minute walk, to get closer to your job, or school, or just to buy a container of low fat milk. If you sit much of the time reading, or at the computer, get up and do some of the movements you've already learned from this book – arm, neck, and shoulder movements, some front or side body bending, or put away some of the clutter that may have accumulated. If you stand a lot, lie down and do leg raises to the front, side and back, or do No. 13-1 from this chapter for thighs and buttocks, or sit-ups, or put your feet up on a chair to relax. While sitting in the bus, car or subway, do additional exercises such as tightening the muscles in an area of the body, holding for 6 seconds, then relaxing; do this for various body parts – the shoulder blades, the buttocks, the abdomen, or the feet.

In the kitchen before preparing dinner, place a tightly closed bottle of dish detergent or two boxes of frozen vegetables in each hand, and pulse the arms as you do knee raises to the front or back, hip lifts to the side, rib shifts to the front or back, or knee bends and heel raises. For a heavier weight use the larger detergent bottle that has a handle and do one arm at a time. By the end of the day many of your muscles will have gotten a workout.

NUTRITION HINT: The American Council on Exercise, the U.S. Department of Agriculture and the American Dietetic Association made comparisons between now and the 1950's and came to the conclusion that maybe we ate more fatty foods back then, but we ate much less. Portions were smaller (and probably plates were smaller, too). We also did more household chores ourselves. Sweeping or scrubbing the floor uses up more calories than a stationery bike. Ten minutes of household chores can use up to 40 calories and it adds up by the end of the week. Preparing your meals also uses up calories, besides which you know exactly what's going into your dinner. We're lucky to have such excellent selections of fruits and vegetables in stores nowadays – some of them even precut and washed. As for the low fat or low sugar cookies or desserts, skip all of those and just have a piece of fruit.

****

No. 13-5 – TWIST AND PRESS

Stand with feet slightly apart and parallel; flat palms on groin.

1-2	Twist the upper torso to the right from the waistline, being careful to keep the hips facing front. At the same time extend the right arm out and press the right flat palm 2 times, toward the back of the room; the elbow bends and extends slightly each time.
3-4	Reverse counts 1-2, pressing the left flat palm toward the back of the room as the upper torso twists toward the left. The right palm is again flat against the groin and the elbow is out to the side.

5-8	Repeat counts 1-4.

9-10 Do a shoulder roll – moving the shoulder forward, up, back and in place – with both flat palms at the groin and the elbows held out to the sides, not back.

11-16 Repeat the shoulder roll 3 times.

17-32 Reverse counts 1-16. The movements are the same; start with the left palm pressing back as the torso twists left. Reverse the shoulder circles – move them back, up, forward and in place.

33-64 Repeat counts 1-32.

FITNESS MINUTES: For a more aerobic exercise, how about trying this at a very lively pace once you know it. Or if you prefer, add some easy jogging in place while you do the torso and arm movements. Watch your space, don't bump into anything.

NUTRITION HINT: A combination of exercise, no smoking, correct weight for your body type and eating proper food is best. Vegetables, fruits, whole grain, nuts, yogurt, skinless chicken, turkey, lean meat, and fish rich in omega-3 fatty acids like wild or canned salmon, trout, halibut, sardine, and mackerel has been proven to be the best preventive measure for many diseases such as obesity, diabetes, Alzheimer's, cancer, high blood pressure, and heart disease. Get the full benefit offered from antioxidants in vegetables and fruits, by eating a variety of them, and not always the same ones. Make an effort to try a new one once a month; then you won't miss out on any of the valuable nutrients they contain. Check out the cookbooks in the Bibliography and ask your library to reserve one for you. They all have delicious recipes; I read all of them and have favorites from each book. Choose simple or complex recipes as suits your taste.

****

No. 13-6 – ELBOW SWING

Start with the fingers curled in front; the right hand is on top and its fingers are hooked onto the fingers of the left hand, which is under with the palm up; the elbows are out at the sides and the shoulders are back.

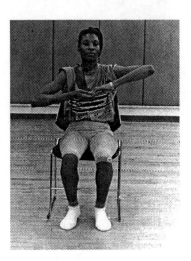

+	Start to swing the elbows toward the right side; the right elbow swings up slightly.
1	The arms finish their swing to the right on count 1.
+2	Reverse and swing the elbows over to the left side.
3-16	Repeat 7 times counts 1+2.
17-24	Relax; shake out the arms and hands down at your sides and get ready to repeat.
25-96	Repeat 3 times, counts 1-24.

This is another exercise you can easily do even while sitting down.

FITNESS MINUTES: Sufficient sleep has been found to be very beneficial for motor skills: piano playing, typing, swimming, bicycling, etc. Eight to nine hours is the recommended amount, but a Japanese study found seven hours to be the very best. Preference is given by all the experts to a regular schedule for getting up and for going to bed. You'll feel more relaxed, better able to concentrate and stay alert.

NUTRITION HINT: Here's another healthy, easy recipe; it's a stew for two and the leftovers are for the next day's lunch or dinner. In a large casserole, spray 1-2 tablespoon of olive oil (or use low fat broth, or water). Add, thinly sliced, 1/2 to 1 onion and 2 cloves of garlic also sliced, your choice of protein – chicken or turkey breast, or low fat beef, veal, lamb or pork, cut in pieces, or skinless chicken drums, and probably a little water. Then add 1/2 a cup of either pearl barley (let it brown in the olive oil), or brown or white rice, lentils or macaroni, or 2 medium-sized thinly sliced potatoes (unpeeled have more vitamins), or yams, peeled. You'll need more liquid if you are using rice or macaroni, so have boiling water ready to add and do use the low-salt liquid from canned vegetables, also, if you wish.

Now add 3 different kinds of vegetables; about 1/2 to 3/4 cup of each; these can be fresh, frozen, leftovers, or canned, low salt. Cut the vegetables in small pieces or use canned, if you are in a hurry. Add spices: basil, oregano, rosemary, parsley, sage, or thyme; try different ones. Also use tomato puree, diced tomatoes or bell peppers, as desired. You can vary the foods used in the recipe and it will be delicious and different each time. Try out different foods, and jot down the combinations you enjoyed most so you can prepare those again. Add more liquid as needed; but if you have a surplus, uncover the casserole when it's almost cooked.

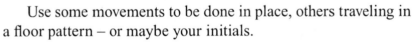

DANCE ROUTINE – CREATIVE MIX

Play a piece you haven't tried yet, or maybe some rock music from the 50's – "Whole Lotta Shakin' Goin' On", Jerry Lee Lewis, 1957.

Consider all the movements in both this chapter and any of the previous ones and use your creativity to put together a varied and fun-to-do mix in this routine.

Use some movements to be done in place, others traveling in a floor pattern – or maybe your initials.

Try an assortment of jumps – stride, chug, twist, skip, hop, light run.

Maybe you remember a turn that you want to put in here.

If you've been practicing with others, then take turns choosing what comes next, or do as the well known modern dance choreographer, Merce Cunningham, has often done – use chance as a method of selection. Write down a different movement on each of 5-10 pieces of paper; place the papers in a bag, pick one out, that's step number one, and so on, and do your routine in that exact order. Tomorrow you can use the same method and come up with a different routine for those same steps. Have fun. You should walk through your new

139

routine before trying it more rapidly, then quicken the pace or run through it; repeat your routine, slow, fast, etc., as often as you can in 2-4 minutes. Try to do it slowly at the end of your time limit and you can use this as your cooling down segment.

FITNESS MINUTES: Each time you put together this routine, give your memory, creativity, and powers of observation a little exercise also. Use favorite movements and vary them to suit yourself; use steps that you've done elsewhere, at some time or other; incorporate your version of sequences you've seen on TV, musicals, or videos. Plan a new routine every time you practice, then choose your favorite. Try to remember them, or just forget them and plan a new one. Use different music: children's pieces, a jazzy rendition of Bach or whatever appeals to you. Plan the routine to a selection and then keep the routine but change the music. Let your children or young relatives or friends put together their own routines and show them to you; then you do one for them. Try these out at the beach, at the park or have a contest to choose the favorite one for that day. The winner gets a tape or CD of a piece of music.

NUTRITION HINT: Vitamins and minerals used to be all-important. They still are but now there are also phytochemicals to consider. These are the latest wonder in nutrition; the majority cannot be gotten from supplements and those that can are considered to be more powerful when eaten in their original plant source together with the other antioxidants to be found there; one must eat colorful fruits and vegetables to avail oneself of the over one thousand phytochemicals found in plants. Plants produce these compounds to protect themselves from the sun or from bugs, and to give their fruit a scent and color. Fruits and vegetables of various colors contain different phytochemicals.

According to research, one tiny blueberry alone contains minute quantities of many minerals and vitamins as well as one hundred varieties of phytochemicals, and that little blueberry can protect your brain, and help fend off arthritis and Alzheimer's. Mother may not have known why, but she was right when she said, "eat all your vegetables and fruits." Whenever you give up empty calories and substitute colorful fruits and vegetables for them you are eating foods that will fight your health battles for you beforehand and each color has many phytochemicals (also called phytonutrients) that look after a certain area of our health. So aim for a wide assortment of colors – rich and varied – in your meals and 30 minutes to one hour of exercise per day for a healthier life.

****

SUGGESTED READING

Blom, Lynne Anne and I. Tarin Chaplin. *The Moment of Movement.* Pittsburgh, Pa.: The University of Pittsburgh Press, 1988.

Consumer Reports on Health. Yonkers, N.Y.: Consumers Union, 2001-2004, Monthly.

Dieckmann, Jane Marsh. *Low Fat One-Dish Meals from around the World.* Freedom, CA: The Crossing Press, 1993.

Jenkins, Nancy Harmon. *The Mediterranean Diet Cookbook, A Delicious Alternative for Lifelong Health.* NY: Bantam Books, 1994.

GLOSSARY

Abductors: Muscles that move a body part away from the center of the body.

Adductors: Muscles that move a body part toward the center of the body.

Aerobics: Activities involving energetic movements; walking, jumping, bicycling, fencing, dancing, gardening, sports, etc. These place a strenuous demand on the cardiovascular system (heart, lungs, blood vessels) and promote cardiovascular fitness by circulating more blood and oxygen to the heart, the brain and throughout the body. An activity that raises your pulse rate and is sustained for 4-5 minutes will develop aerobic power.

Alexander technique: A relaxation technique based on body awareness and imagery. It can help solve balance and coordination problems, help align the body for better posture, and increase range of motion.

Alignment: Posture.

Allicin: It is found in the onion family: leeks, scallions, and onions. It has antitumor properties. Allin in garlic converts to allicin upon being crushed or chopped.

Allspice: A spice with antibiotic powers.

Allylic sulfides: These are antioxidants found in plants of the lily family – onions, garlic, leeks, chives – that give them their odor. They can help lower blood pressure, heighten immunity, decrease risk of some cancers, lower cholesterol and triglyceride levels, and they have antibiotic properties. Research has shown that garlic, cooked or raw, releases more antioxidants when cut fine or crushed than whole.

Alpha-carotene: It belongs to the carotenoid group of phytochemicals; it is an antioxidant that inhibits cancer and is prevalent mostly in orange foods: carrots, cantaloupes, bananas, winter squash and pumpkins.

Anterior: The front part of the body.

Anthocyanins: These are antioxidants that help to delay cellular aging, have potent anti-inflammatory effects, reduce platelet clumping and thus assist the heart by blocking the formation of blood clots. They are to be found in foods in the red/purple group: cherries, blueberries, blackberries, grapes, red wine, plums, prunes, strawberries, raspberries, cranberries, pomegranates, currants, red apples and red onions, red cabbage, eggplants, but not beets. There are more anthocyanins in raw foods, since heating damages them.

Antioxidants: They assist in absorbing free radicals (toxic molecules produced by the body). Since the antioxidants carry an extra electron, they are able to give one to free radicals that lack one and are very destructive, thus inhibiting their destructive activity. According to Ronald Prior, Ph.D., chief of the phytochemical laboratory at the U.S. Department of Agriculture's Arkansas Children's Nutrition Center, the most potent antioxidants are to be found in blueberries, blackberries, strawberries, oranges, and cranberries, while the leading vegetables are kale, asparagus, watercress, spinach, and red peppers when you compare standard serving sizes.

Ascorbic Acid: See Vitamin C.

Ball change: Same as a catch step. It was named after the only steps that could possibly be done outdoors by prisoners working while tied to a ball and chain – a small step to relieve the foot with the ball tied to it, then a larger step either to the front, side, or back with the free foot.

Ballistic stretch: Involves bouncing, pulsing repetitive movements executed to stretch a muscle. Gentle pulses are all right; fierce ones are not.

Basil: An herb containing the antioxidants beta carotene and lutein as well as calcium, potassium, iron and magnesium.

Bay leaves: A spice which helps make insulin more competent and assists in keeping insulin levels regular.

Beans: Excellent source of proteins, fiber and an assortment of minerals and vitamins. (See flatulence.) They help to lower the cholesterol level and to keep blood sugar levels steady.

Beta-carotene: Another member of the carotenoid group of phytochemicals; it is an antioxidant and is one of the forms of carotene that is widely found in nature, especially in orange and dark green foods – in carrots, tomatoes, broccoli, mangoes, turnip greens, spinach, kale, sweet potatoes, red bell peppers, winter squash, apricots, apples, and cantaloupes. However, it needs to be eaten with a little fat, e.g., olive oil or yogurt, in order for the body to absorb the beta-carotene. It can help prevent cancer, by protecting cells in the body against oxidation damage by free radicals, by scooping them up and also by generating other antioxidants; what's more, it can also be converted to Vitamin A as needed. There is little loss of carotenes in cooking since they are almost insoluble in water.

Betacyanins: The rich red pigment from beets. Although beets are red, they have no anthocyanins; they have betaine which assists in detoxifying homocysteine, an amino acid that, in excess, can lead to heart disease.

Betaine: See betacyanins.

Biotin: A nutrient easily found in foods. It is concerned with energy metabolism.

Blood pressure: Ideally should be less than 120/80. The first number is the systolic pressure, the force of blood pushing against the arteries as the heart pumps. The second number is the diastolic pressure – the measure of force between heartbeats.

Boron: A mineral that is found in apples and is important for the brain and for calcium metabolism.

Brush: The foot stretches along the floor with the leg straight till you get to your pointed toes, then relax the ankle and return the foot in place with a straight leg, by relaxing the instep. The tip of the toe remains on the floor throughout.

Calcium: It is found in dairy foods, as well as in broccoli, kidney beans, dark green leafy vegetables, fish with edible soft bones such as canned salmon and sardines, figs, almonds, tofu, yogurt and low fat frozen yogurt; the body absorbs it more easily from food than from supplements. Calcium is absorbed well from sardines, canned salmon, bok choy, and kale, but poorly from spinach and Swiss chard which are high in the calcium-blocking substances oxalate and phytate. With age it is easier for people to absorb calcium citrate supplements, which do not require acid secretions by the stomach lining, than calcium carbonate supplements. A lack of calcium can cause the bones to become thin and lead to osteoporosis, fractures and loss of mobility and perhaps lead to the suppression of the breakdown of fat and encourage fat storage. Calcium builds bones and teeth, regulates heart rhythm, is important to the skin, lowers blood pressure and helps prevent colon cancer. The usual daily calcium intake goal is 1,000 to 1,500 milligrams spread out throughout the day. It is essential for nerve activity, muscle contraction and blood clotting. Excess can cause constipation and impair iron absorption and kidney function.

Calories: A unit of energy-producing potential equal to the amount of heat that is contained in food and released upon oxidation by the body.

Cardamon: A spice with strong antioxidant properties.

Carotenoids: A family of antioxidants that includes lutein, zeaxanthin, lycopene and beta-carotene and is found in butternut squash, red bell peppers, cantaloupes, apricots, carrots, tomatoes, broccoli, turnip greens and spinach. For better absorption by the body, they should be eaten with meat or foods with a little oil.

Cataract: A clouding of the lens of the eye, which reduces visual sharpness, produces an overall haze, diminished detail and sensitivity to glare. The antioxidants lutein and zeaxanthin found in spinach, corn and egg yolks help reduce the incidence of cataracts. Wearing a hat and sunglasses is protection from ultraviolet rays (UV), which are linked to cataracts and macular degeneration.

Catechins: They are a flavanol and belong to the flavonoid group of antioxidants. They neutralize free radicals in the body; they also protect DNA and blood vessels from damage by oxidants, and may protect arteries from plaque build-up. They are found in tea, especially green tea.

Cayenne pepper: A spice with antibiotic powers.

Celery: A good source of 3-n-butyl phthalide, a compound that helps to lower blood pressure.

Centered: An awareness of the position of the body so that both sides are similarly placed or there is an inner feeling of balance in the body.

Charley horse: A cramp or stiffness in a muscle, caused by strain.

Chippendale exercising chair: An 18th century English furniture style marked by flowing lines and rococo ornamentation, and named after the British cabinetmaker, Thomas Chippendale; this style was used in the exercising chairs of that time.

Cholesterol: A certain amount of cholesterol is needed by the body for the production of brain tissue, digestive juices, some hormones, vitamin D and the bile acids necessary for digesting fat. Too much fat in the diet leads to more LDL, less HDL and a greater possibility of health problems. Heredity, genes, weight, and exercise are also a factor in this. The aim is less than 200 total cholesterol, no higher than 100 LDL, and an HDL of 50 or more. The body does produce the amount it needs, so an excess supply occurs when people eat too much saturated fat and hydrogenated fat. This excess is the bad cholesterol – LDL, low-density lipoprotein – that accumulates in the arteries, clogs them up and can increase the possibility of heart attacks, strokes and cerebral thrombosis when a clot occurs in a blood vessel in the brain.

Choline: It is an essential nutrient found in eggs, beef liver, beef, cauliflower, grape juice, potatoes with the skin, and in whole milk. It plays an important role in maintaining and developing the ability to think and remember. As with everything, moderation is best since excess can cause damage.

Chromium: A mineral – a trace element – found in yeast, beer, liver, beef, chicken, broccoli, mushrooms, and cereals. It is contained in all tissues concerned with glucose metabolism.

Chug: A sliding or very small jumping movement, either to the front or to the back and usually on two feet.

Cinnamon: Helps maintain blood sugar levels by making insulin more efficient in processing sugar. Half a teaspoon daily helps lower fasting blood sugar level and LDL – bad cholesterol – by nearly 20 percent and triglycerides, potentially artery-clogging fat, by about 25 percent according to the Beltsville Human Nutrition Research Center in Maryland and Richard Anderson, Ph.D., of the U.S. Department of Agriculture. It's excellent on cereal, fruit, hot chocolate, and coffee.

Clove: A spice that, like cinnamon, turmeric and bay leaf, assists in normalizing blood sugar through its reaction on insulin.

Cobalamin: See Vitamin B-12.

Cobalt: A trace mineral found in liver and other meat. It is indispensable for the formation of red blood cells.

Coffee: Strong roasts, whether decaf or regular, contain antioxidants that boost up the enzymes to protect against colon cancer.

Collagen: The underlying tissue network that maintains the tone and structure of the skin, helps to heal wounds, and keeps capillary walls and blood vessels strong.

Complete protein: Proteins containing good amounts of all the necessary amino acids, e.g., most animal and legume proteins.

Contract and release: The muscle shortens and thickens as it contracts; on the release the muscle relaxes.

Contraction: The shortening and thickening of a functioning muscle or muscle fiber.

Cooling down: A slow, relaxed movement done after strenuous activity to allow the heart to begin to circulate the blood to the muscles in a more normal manner after having helped you to exercise strenuously by sending an increased supply of blood throughout the body. The cooling down movement should be centered, slow and relaxed.

Copper: A mineral – a trace element – found in green vegetables, barley, nuts, beans, potatoes, whole grains, fish and liver. It is necessary for hemoglobin formation and is a constituent of many enzymes.

Core Conditioning: It is an integrated approach and focuses its attention on developing the muscles of the center of the body, such as the trunk, the spine, torso, back, inner and outer thighs, together with correct breathing and posture and muscle awareness. Pilates and yoga are based on core conditioning.

Coriander: A spice that has antioxidant properties.

Cross training: Involves varying your exercise program by training in 2 or 3 different kinds of workouts, thus using more varied muscle groups and in different ways, e.g., kick boxing, swimming and the workouts from this book. It adds variety to the workouts, decreases the likelihood of overusing or underutilizing any muscles, and prevents the muscles from getting into the habit of doing a set regime of movements, resulting in little gain and much boredom. The results of research at Johns Hopkins suggests that the number and variety of physical activity – gardening, cycling, walking, swimming, and bowling – may be more important for the elderly than the frequency or intensity of an activity, because more areas of the brain are kept active.

Cruciferous vegetables: They are in the cabbage family, such as Brussels sprouts, broccoli, bok choy, kale and cauliflower. These, as well as turnips and watercress (mustard family) belong to the green group of vegetables and are rich in vitamin C, beta-carotene, phytochemicals, fiber, and antioxidants that stimulate the genes in the liver to turn on the manufacture of enzymes that break down cancer-causing chemicals in the body.

Cumin: A spice with strong, antioxidant properties as well as antibiotic powers.

Curcumin: A spice that is being studied as a possible treatment for pancreatic cancer and for multiple myeloma; it may cause cancer cells to stop proliferating and cause malignant tumors to self-destruct, according to scientists at M.D. Anderson Center in Houston. It may also be beneficial in fighting the accumulation of destructive protein in the brain and the inflammation that may contribute to Alzheimer's, according to researchers at the Alzheimer's Disease Research Center at the University of California, Los Angeles.

Dash Diet: (Dash stands for Dietary Approaches to Stop Hypertension) It has proven to be very successful in stopping hypertension. In general it emphasizes low sodium intake, only low fat dairy, up to ten servings of fruits and vegetables a day, and approximately 5 servings of nuts and legumes a week. It is not a diet for losing weight, but since fewer calories seem to be consumed it can be a good way to lose weight. For a free booklet, call 1-301-592-8573.

Dehydration: Reduction of the water content of the body.

Diabetes: A metabolic disorder in which too much sugar accumulates in the bloodstream rather than entering the cells throughout the body; the body is not producing enough insulin, the hormone that enables it to digest starches and sugars. Those suffering from diabetes must be sure not to eat more carbohydrates than they can digest.

DNA: is short for the chemical (deoxyribonucleic acid) that makes up the human genome which determines, or rather, defines who you are and does so in every single cell in your body. Cancer and many other diseases are caused by damage to your DNA. Phytochemicals found in fruits and vegetables help protect your DNA.

Double hip lift: Two consecutive hip lifts to the same side; after doing one hip lift to the right the hip returns halfway to center, lifts again to the right and then returns to center.

Double time: Twice as fast.

Downstage: The front of the stage. The term dates back to the time when most stages were raked – on an angle – with the back high and the front low, so the audience could see everyone on the stage even if the seats were all on the same level. Performers had to walk downhill to get to the front of the stage.

Endurance: The ability to perform a muscular contraction many times in rapid succession. Training increases the endurance of particular muscle groups.

Fat soluble vitamins: These vitamins are A, D, E and K.

Fats: See: Cholesterol, HDL, High-density lipoproteins, Hydrogenation, LDL, Low-density lipoproteins, Monounsaturated fats, Omega-3 fatty acids, Partially hydrogenated fats, Polyunsaturated fats, Saturated fats, Stearic acid, Triglycerides. All fats, good or bad, are about 140 calories per tablespoon.

Fiber: There are 2 kinds: Insoluble dietary fiber, called roughage, is the cellulose and lignin found around whole grains and fruit and vegetable skins. It absorbs water as it goes through the body; this lowers the possibility of constipation by moving food quickly through the intestinal tract and perhaps helps prevent colon cancer. Soluble dietary fiber dissolves in water and is found in the flesh of fruits and vegetable such as apples, pears, grapefruit, barley, carrots and beans, and in the gums and pectin in sticky foods such as oatmeal and oat bran cereals. The bulk fills you up and helps to prevent hunger pangs by keeping your blood-sugar level constant. This soluble fiber also absorbs cholesterol and rids the body of it.

Flamenco: A dance style of the Spanish Andalusian Gypsies, characterized by forceful and improvised music.

Flatback: The torso is bent forward and is parallel to the floor and flat like a table.

Flatulence from beans: Gas. The sugars – raffinose and stachyose – in beans are the cause. To avoid this from canned beans, throw away the liquid, rinse the beans many times. When you cook dried beans, after the water with the beans has boiled, throw away the water, place your beans in fresh boiling water and go on with your recipe.

Flavanols: Are a subset of flavonoids and include quercetin, kaempferol and catechins.

Flavonoids: These antioxidants are found in dark chocolate and in both green and black tea, buckwheat, nuts of all sorts, as well as in fruits and vegetables. They raise the level of good cholesterol in the body and act as an antioxidant to neutralize free radicals in the body, inhibit blood clotting, and protect blood vessels and DNA that could be damaged by oxidants. These particular flavonoids are called catechins. Flavonoids also help protect against chronic diseases such as lung cancer, prostate cancer, asthma, and type 2 diabetes. Those in the white/green group of foods are called quercetin (apples – the skin – and onions) and kaempferol (white cabbage), maringenin (citrus fruits), and myricetin (berries). There exist more than 4,000 flavonoid compounds in numerous subgroups, all with different names. Flavonoids are linked with the safeguarding of cardiovascular health. They are scavengers of free radicals.

Flexibility: The ability of the joints of the body to go through their full range of motion safely and comfortably.

Flexion: A bending movement of a body part.

Flicking: A sharp throwing movement – as in a leg kick, or a hand throw from the arm and wrist with long extended fingers.

Floor design: The design made on the floor when executing a movement: walking in a square, a triangle, a figure 8, a letter B, etc.

Fluoride: A mineral found in sea fish (mackerel, salmon), and in water in minute quantities. It is often added to drinking water if the fluorine content is low. It is vital for teeth and bone health. It is beneficial in hindering tooth decay and hardens tooth enamel by combining with calcium phosphate to form calcium fluorapatite.

Folate (called folic acid in supplements and fortified foods): A member of the B vitamins (B-9) that is found in leafy green vegetables such as spinach, collard greens, green cabbage, kale, Swiss chard, broccoli, lentils, bananas, oranges, boysenberries, dried beans and peas, beets, asparagus, artichoke, potatoes, yeast, liver, nuts and seeds, and is always added to flour. It prevents neural-tube defects in babies, lowers blood levels of homocysteine, an amino acid that aggravates blood vessels and is linked to heart disease and it helps to synthesize DNA required for new cells. It may likewise reduce the risk of hypertension in women. A deficiency of folate and Vitamin B-12 is also associated with hearing problems in the aged.

Free radicals: Toxic materials produced by the body as a byproduct of our daily activities: digesting and/or breathing various compounds such as medications, rancid fats, hydrogenated oils, inhaled components of air pollution, and other damaging sources.

Beta-carotene and vitamins C and E, with strong antioxidant properties, function as free radical scavengers; they have the ability to oppose and quench free radicals.

Gingerols and diarylhaptanoids: These phytochemicals have strong antioxidant activity and are found in ginger. According to scientific research, they thin the blood, help reduce pain, are anti-inflammatory and have antinausea properties.

Glutathione: An important antioxidant that the body can easily generate as needed, but not necessarily so when we get older. It is found in spinach, asparagus, winter squash, potatoes, avocado, oranges, grapefruits and strawberries. It is best preserved in raw or stir-fried foods, not in boiled foods. It detoxifies pollutants and carcinogens, helps keep the liver healthy, reduces chronic inflammation, helps keep the immune system working efficiently and helps lower blood pressure and cholesterol levels.

Gluteus maximus: The muscle found from the middle of the buttocks to the side of the hip; it helps to straighten the leg after sitting; it lifts the leg away from the body.

Gluteus medius and gluteus minimus: Muscles found at the top and sides of the buttocks; they lift the leg up at the side, away from the body.

Glycemic load: Measures how rapidly a carbohydrate is digested. Sweets, white bread, white potatoes and canned fruits in heavy syrup are easily and quickly digested and have a high glycemic load, meaning they can cause blood sugar levels to rise quickly; this is a concern for those who are insulin resistant or have diabetes. Pasta, whole wheat, lentils, legumes are digested slowly and thus are healthy for your heart; they have a low glycemic load.

Half time: Half as fast.

Hamstrings: Muscles at the back of the thighs involved with knee flexion and thigh extension.

HDL: High-density lipoproteins, or "good" cholesterol. They carry cholesterol from the tissues to the liver.

Heat stroke: A combination of hyperthermia and dehydration.

Hesperetin: A flavanol that lowers inflammation, reduces hypertension, diminishes bad cholesterol while augmenting the good one.

High-density lipoproteins: "good" cholesterol (HDL) prevents buildup of fatty tissue in the arteries; it transports cholesterol to be metabolized as bile salts by the liver and eliminated from the body harmlessly, through the intestinal tract.

High-fructose corn syrup: It may cause weight gain, slow burning of fat and elevate the level of "bad" cholesterol. It is well liked by manufacturers: it has a long shelf life, is not expensive, and keeps foods from drying out. Its use includes processed foods, ketchup and bread.

High impact aerobics: Consists of jumps, brisk lively movement executed continuously for half an hour at a time.

Hinge: A movement involving bending back in a straight line from the knees to the top of the head, usually while kneeling.

Hook lying position: Knees are bent and pointing up while lying on the back with feet flat on the floor.

Homocysteine: An amino acid that the body uses to build and maintain tissues. In excess it may hasten damage to arteries. Luckily folic acid, a B Vitamin, helps to depress this amino acid. Folic acid can be found in green leafy vegetables, dried beans and orange juice.

Hula: A Polynesian dance with undulating hips and miming movements of the hands and arms.

Hydrogenation: The process used by manufacturers to transform vegetable oils in packaged foods so that the packaged food will be more shelf stable. This creates trans fats and partially hydrogenated fats, both of which are bad fats; they are found in some cereals, cookies, doughnuts, etc.

Hyper extended legs: Legs that curve out toward the back.

Hypertension: It is caused by a persistent high blood pressure. Its parameters are defined as: a systolic blood pressure of 140 or more, and a diastolic pressure of 90 or more. If either number rises there is increased risk of developing heart and blood vessel diseases. Hypertension affects blood vessels to the heart, brain, kidney, and eyes. A more active lifestyle and less salt in the daily diet are usually recommended. Fresh produce is less salty than processed, so it is also preferable.

Hyperthermia: Abnormally high body temperature.

Hypothermia: Unusually low body temperature.

Imagery: A mental picture, which assists one in achieving a better execution of a step or position.

Indoles: Antioxidants that help to prevent breast cancer and other cancers. They are found in cruciferous vegetable, such as broccoli, Brussels sprouts, and kale when these vegetables are steamed rather than cooked in lots of water.

Iodine: A mineral essential in small amounts to prevent goiter characterized by a swollen neck or goiter; it is a component of thyroid hormones. It is found in drinking water, seaweeds, seafoods such as cod, salmon, herring, and in "iodized salt".

Iron: It is an important mineral for children, infants and pregnant women. It is necessary for the formation of hemoglobin, which stores oxygen in red blood cells. Heme iron is found in lean red meat, organ meats, pork, beef, egg yolks, (from which it is easily absorbed); non heme iron is found in dark green vegetables, peas, beets, legumes, cream of wheat, wheat germ and oat bran. The iron from these is not as easily released to the body and is more available if eaten together with either tomatoes or a vitamin C-rich food such as the addition of lemon juice. However, if taken in excess by children, or by those with some hereditary conditions, it can be very dangerous.

Isolation: Movement of individual body parts such as the ribs, hips, shoulders and head.

Isometrics: Involves a static contraction of a muscle against an immovable force: wall, floor, legs of a chair, etc., with an increase in muscle tension but without a change of muscle length.

Isothiocyanates: These phytochemicals, which inhibit cancer, are found in broccoli and other cruciferous vegetables.

Isotonic: A type of muscular contraction in which the length of the muscle changes.

Jazz hand: A very tense, widely stretched hand with all the fingers fully extended.

Kickboxing: Kickboxing originated from the martial art of karate. The Japanese boxing promoter Osamu Noguchi used this term for a variant of karate that he created in 1950. However, unlike karate, no shins, knees or elbows are allowed. It is similar to boxing but utilizes the feet and legs as well as the hands. It provides a workout with athletic movements good for burning calories and sculpting the body; many people like this workout for cross training.

Kneeovers: Dropping of the knees over to one side or the other, either while sitting or lying on the back, without moving the upper torso.

Knee pop: From a standing, straight leg position, lift the heels so that the knees bend sharply without moving the rest of the body.

LDL: Low-density lipoproteins, or "bad" cholesterol – a form of lipoprotein that is rich in the form of cholesterol that is carried to the tissues and may cause risk of heart disease.

Legumes: They are rich in proteins, soluble fiber, vitamins, minerals, and antioxidants and include dried beans, peas and lentils.

Leptin: A hormone that may be important in controlling hunger. As you sleep, the amount of leptin in your body increases and results in lower feelings of hunger. Lack of sleep seems to result in preventing the rise of leptin and increasing the feeling of hunger.

Lift: To raise the isolated portion of the body, i.e., shoulders or hips.

Limenoids: Phytochemicals found in citrus fruits; they inhibit cancer.

Lipoprotein: (Lp) a cholesterol-carrying molecule similar in structure to LDL. It contributes to atherosclerosis (hardening of the arteries) and may increase the risk of blood clots. Fats are transported in the blood as lipoproteins.

Long-legged sitting: Sitting on the floor with straight legs together, directly in front of the hips.

Low-density lipoproteins: LDL, or "bad" cholesterol can cause heart attacks and strokes by blocking the arteries.

Low impact aerobics: Any continuous movement without jumps or very brisk action.

Lunge: Large step on a bent leg, usually to the front or side.

Lutein: An antioxidant found in the yellow/green group of vegetables such as corn, egg yolk (chickens eat corn), broccoli, kiwifruit, avocados, red bell peppers, tangerines, honeydew melon and green leafy vegetables like kale, parsley, watercress, collard, and spinach; it may help fight against macular degeneration, and reduces the risk of cataracts.

Lycopene: A powerful antioxidant in the carotenoid group that turns vegetables and fruits dark orange and is found in guava, watermelon, cooked red tomatoes, canned tomatoes, and ketchup; it fights cancer, helps to prevent UV (ultraviolet) damage, and protects the lungs from oxidative damage. Cooking actually boosts the lycopene content in tomatoes.

Macular degeneration: Degeneration of the eyes that occurs with aging, when the macula – the central portion of the eye that is in charge of color, detail and daylight vision – is damaged; it can be prevented to some extent by the antioxidants zeaxanthin and lutein that are found in spinach, egg yolks and corn. Harvard researchers found that fats from fish and nuts also seemed to reduce the risk of macular degeneration. Sunglasses and wide brimmed hats are suggested as protection from ultraviolet rays, which may cause this. Eating spinach is good too. Zinc, copper, and the three antioxidants, vitamin C, E, and beta-carotene are also beneficial.

Magnesium: It is found in grapefruit and orange juice, bananas, fish, chicken, nuts, spinach, peanut butter, whole grains, legumes, artichoke, avocado, green vegetables, meat (animals eat grass), cashews and hard drinking water (it contains minerals); it is important if calcium is to work to capacity for strong bones and for the prevention of osteoporosis. It helps lower blood pressure, keep the heart rhythm steady, control blood sugar and maintain correct muscle and nerve function. Taking it in excess is dangerous for those with impaired kidney function.

Manganese: A trace mineral found in tea, cereals, beans, and nuts. It forms part of some enzyme systems in the body.

Mediterranean diet: Consists of many varied fruits and vegetables, whole grains, unsaturated vegetable oils, olive oil and proteins derived from fish, beans and chicken, and little if any red meat.

Metabolism: The total of all physical and chemical processes by which the human body is maintained.

Minerals: They are consumed in food and good for you, unless taken in excess in supplements. Some of the important ones are calcium, magnesium, iron, zinc and selenium.

Molybdenum: A trace mineral important in enzyme activation. It is found in kidney, cereals and vegetables in small amounts.

Monoterpenes: These are phytonutrients that help prevent cancer by blocking some of the cancer-causing compounds. They are found in cherries and in the peel of citrus fruits.

Monounsaturated fats: Good fats that are found in olive, canola, nut and avocado oils and the foods from which these oils come, such as walnuts. Substitution of good fats for bad fats leads to lower levels of harmful cholesterol, less threat of diabetes and of heart problems.

Neurotransmitter: A chemical messenger within the brain that allows communication between nerve cells.

Niacin: See Vitamin B-3. Vital for the metabolism of carbohydrates, fats and proteins, it is essential for healthy skin, the nervous system and the digestive tract.

Nutmeg: A spice with antibiotic properties.

Nutrient: Any element or compound contributing to or necessary for an organism's metabolism, growth or other function. Those providing energy are carbohydrates, proteins, and fat. Those sustaining metabolism are minerals, vitamins, and water. Phytonutrients, organic compounds from plants, are the latest discovery in nutrients. Many nutrients cannot be synthesized by the body and must be obtained directly from a food source.

Nutrient deficiency: Appears mostly in those who eat a limited variety of foods, and especially among the elderly.

Omega-3 fatty acids: A special kind of fat, found in algae, which fish finally get to as large fish feed on smaller, etc. These fats may reduce the risk of heart attacks. They prevent platelets from clumping together as plaques against the walls of the arteries; prevent abnormal heart rhythms that are often the cause of sudden cardiac deaths. They lower the triglycerides level, may also help prevent Alzheimer's and keep depression away. They are found in wild Pacific salmon, shrimp, (farmed shrimp are fed a vegetable paste, so they are equal to white chicken meat in cholesterol content – very little), haddock, lake trout, albacore tuna, herring, mackerel, bluefish, canned sardines, canned salmon, hake whiting, rainbow smelt, as well as in walnuts, flaxseed, canola (rapeseed), pumpkin seeds, dark green vegetables and soybean oil. The Harvard School of Public Health recommends two meals of fish per week, a different kind each time.

Omega-6 fatty acids: They are found in corn, sesame and sunflower oil. The amount of omega-6 oil intake is usually sufficient. The omega-3 are much more important for a healthy diet.

Oregano: A spice with strong antioxidant properties providing anti-diabetic and antibiotic benefits.

Organ meats: These include heart, liver, spleen and sweetbreads. They are high in cholesterol content, should not be eaten often, and even then only in small portions.

Osteoporosis: Bone atrophy; involves a reduction of bone mass. When the bones carry the weight of the body on a daily basis, during exercise, the cells build more bone – dense and strong. If the calcium intake is insufficient the bone breakdown is faster than the increase of bone mass. Magnesium, potassium, Vitamin D as well as calcium are necessary for bone strength. The Framingham Osteoporosis Study discovered that a diet high in fruits and vegetables seemed to be protective against osteoporosis in men.

Pantothenic acid: It is also known as Vitamin B-5 and is a nutrient found in fruits, vegetables, meats, fish, legumes and whole grain cereals. It is involved with energy metabolism and helps protect the body from stress.

Parsley: An herb in cooking; besides adding flavor it serves as a digestive aid and mild diuretic.

Partially hydrogenated fats: These, like saturated fats, are bad for you; they increase the likelihood of heart disease. They occur when hydrogenation is used to increase the shelf life of packaged foods.

Passive stretch: Same as static stretch; a slow controlled stretch involving the use of a held position; 20-30 seconds is recommended for lengthening the muscle, while more could lead to injury.

Pathogenic: Capable of causing disease.

Pectin: A soluble fiber found in apples, plums, peaches, and pears. It promotes a feeling of satiety by keeping your blood-sugar level stable by binding sugars, to keep them from entering the blood all at the same time. Pectin also lowers cholesterol by mopping it and bile salts in the digestive tract and sending them out of the body.

Phenolics: A group of protective antioxidant phytochemicals that activate cancer-fighting enzymes. They are found in tomatoes, grapes and wine, green and black teas, cereal grains, fruits and vegetables.

Phosphorus: A mineral essential for soft tissue and bone growth and normal function. It is necessary for energy storage and transfer, cell division and reproduction. It is found in dried beans, eggs, meat, poultry and fish.

Phthalides: Phytochemicals that inhibit cancer and are found in celery seeds.

Phytosterols: Antioxidants found in large amounts in nuts of all kinds, seeds, whole wheat, cucumbers, corn and soybeans. They help lower the cholesterol level and are cancer inhibitors.

Phytochemicals: (also called phytonutrients) are disease-fighting chemicals found only in fruits and vegetables. There are an endless variety of these, which is why nutritionists now recommend 9 rather than 5-9 servings of varieties of fruits and vegetables per day. One serving is about 1/2 cup.

Phytonutrients: A name also given to phytochemicals because they are so good for you. They are not actually nutrients but chemicals and are only found in plant sources. They have an active role in the normal functioning of the body.

Pilates: A popular workout system that emphasizes posture, alignment and form by strengthening the core area of the body, the back, abs, hips and butt, thus creating a "corset" of muscles.

Placement: Alignment.

Plié: A ballet term for bending the knees.

Polychlorinated biphenyls: (PCBs) Cancer causing contaminants. Any of a family of industrial chemical compounds produced by chlorination of biphenyls; noted as an environmental pollutant that accumulates in animal tissue with pathogenic and teratogenic effects.

Polyphenolics: A large class of very strong antioxidants that include flavonoids. And flavonoids include antioxidants in the anthocyanin group. All of these are phytochemicals. It's like a family tree. They may protect against cancer and heart disease.

Polyphenols: Plant chemicals thought to play a role in preventing cancer. Antioxidants such as quercetin in apples are mostly polyphenols. Red Delicious apples rank first among apples in antioxidant power, especially the peel.

Polyunsaturated fat: It is generally a liquid fat, a good fat found in soybean, corn, sunflower, mustard, nuts, grains, fish, vegetables and safflower. They are not as good for you as monounsaturated fats, but they are certainly better than trans fats or saturated fats. Polyunsaturated fats tend to reduce both the bad LDL fats and the good HDL fats in your body. When these fats were used to replace saturated fats, Harvard researchers found that cholesterol levels of LDL dropped, insulin sensitivity improved and the possibility of diabetes was lessened. However, the best fats are olive, walnut, avocado and omega-3 fatty acids.

Potassium: It is a mineral found in bananas, orange juice, apricots, potatoes, tomatoes, and fruits and vegetables but not as plentiful in canned foods. It helps control blood pressure, helps control plaque formation in arteries, and is essential for bone strength. But like many minerals and vitamins, an excess of it is not desirable.

Prance: These are a small running type of movement with the feet pointed.

Proanthocyanidins: These are compounds found in blueberries, cherries and blackberries; they help strengthen the walls of the capillary veins, thus possibly preventing hemorrhoids.

Prone position: Lying down with the frontal area – abdomen – down on the floor.

Pulse: A body accent, small and bouncy.

Pyridoxine: See Vitamin B-6.

Quadriceps: Muscles at the front of the thighs involved with knee extension and thigh flexion.

Quercetin: A phytochemical, antioxidant flavonoid found in foods in the white/green color group such as green grapes, pears, leeks, celery, apples, red and yellow onions, string beans, kale, broccoli, whole grain cereals, buckwheat, and green tea. Research shows that it may help reduce stomach cancer; it is an excellent antioxidant, a natural antihistamine and it also fights inflammation, but it needs to be backed up by other phytochemicals from the plant source rather than be taken as a supplement.

Raked stage: A stage that slants, with the back area much higher than the front area.

Release: To relax a muscle after a contraction.

Relevé: Rising to the balls of the feet – a ballet term.

Resistance exercise: Involves the increasing or decreasing of muscle length as an outside resistance – medicine ball, elastic band, or your own body – is resisted and moved through space.

Resveratrol: A phytochemical, an antioxidant known as a polyphenol, found in both nuts, chocolate and wine; it boosts the level of good cholesterol, helps prevent blood clotting and damage to cells, curbs tumor growth and skin cancer, may help prevent hardening of the arteries, thereby decreasing strokes and heart attacks. It can sponge up free radicals and prevent inflammation. Although it can help to stop tumor growth, alcohol has been blamed for causing cirrhosis of the liver and some forms of cancer, so if there is a history of cancer in your family, eat nuts and grapes, and drink grape juice and nonalcoholic wine instead. These have the same antioxidants, but not as much of them. Red wine and grapes are said to be better for you than green grapes or white wine.

Retinol: See Vitamin A.

Riboflavin: See Vitamin B-2.

Rock and roll: A strongly accented two-beat jazz style characterized by a simple melodic line usually based on the blues, easy arrangements for small groups such as rhythm and saxophone, harsh rowdy tones and lyrics dealing with adolescent love.

Rosemary: A spice with strong antioxidant properties. It also helps stimulate appetite.

Rutin: an antioxidant that helps prevent platelets from clumping together and cause clotting. It also shrinks particles of low-density lypoprotein, thus reducing the risk of heart attack and strokes. It is found in buckwheat.

Saffron: A spice containing strong antioxidant properties.

Sage: A spice with antioxidant properties. It may improve the memory of people with Alzheimer's disease.

Salt (Sodium): A mineral that regulates body fluids and is important in the transmission of nerve impulses to send signals to activate your muscles and organs together with potassium. Eating too much of it has been linked to high blood pressure and can cause the loss of calcium which could then increase the risk of osteoporosis. Salt is found naturally in many foods but even more in processed foods, e.g., canned vegetables, soups, and deli meats. Check labels for sodium quantity. Other high-sodium foods include most packaged foods, snacks, bottled spaghetti sauce, fast foods, and even breakfast cereals. People who do very strenuous activity for prolonged periods of time in excessively hot weather, however, may have to take salt tablets to replace salt lost in heavy perspiration.

Samba: A Brazilian dance in which the torso typically sways to the front or back in opposition to the footwork.

Saponins: A chemical that helps to reduce cholesterol levels by binding with cholesterol in the body and then removing it from the body. Saponins may neutralize cancer-causing substances in the intestines. They are found in eggplant, asparagus, potatoes, spinach, tomatoes, and most abundantly in soybeans, chickpeas, barley, oats, and other legumes.

Saturated fat: The fat that is hard at room temperature, such as is found in animal sources: red meat, poultry, cheese, butter and whole milk as well as in tropical oils: coconut, palm kernel, and cocoa butter. They raise the level of cholesterol, which when found in large amounts in the blood serum can block up the arteries and lead to life-threatening clots. They are not good as part of a steady diet.

Scoliosis: A lateral (side) curvature of the spine.

Selenium: A mineral antioxidant found in large quantity in Brazil nuts, walnuts, grains, garlic, eggs, meat, oysters and tuna, according to the U.S. Dept. of Agriculture. It may help to protect the skin from sun-related damage, and it protects healthy cells from damage by free radicals that could cause cancer and heart disease; it enhances one's mood, and is found in most multivitamin supplements. Excess can cause damage to hair and nails, gastrointestinal distress, and slower mental function.

Serotonin: A complex neurotransmitter, an organic compound found in the brain, blood serum and gastric mucous membranes and active in the transmission of nerve impulses. It is synthesized in the central nervous system and in the gastrointestinal tract. Serotonin molecules change the electrical state of a cell. This change can then cause a chemical message to be passed, or inhibited. Excess serotonin molecules are taken back and reprocessed. Serotonin helps in regulating mood, behavior, sleep, sex, and appetite. Certain foods, such as chocolate, and honey, help raise the level of serotonin in the brain. Others will do the same more gradually; these are foods that are digested more slowly like complex carbohydrates – whole wheat bread or pretzels, cereals, brown rice, and legumes – as well as those containing certain protein amino acids (tyrosine, found in almonds, beans and cheddar cheese and low fat cottage cheese, or triptophen, found in turkey, canned tuna and salmon, ham and skim milk). These will take longer to digest and to get into the bloodstream. The safest way to raise serotonin levels is with exercise and a healthy diet that includes complex carbohydrates. Excess can be dangerous.

Shifting: Moving a body part, such as the ribs, directly to the front, side or back.

Shoulder roll: Shoulders circle or roll forward, up, back, and down, or in the reverse direction.

Slides: A smooth jumpy movement traveling either to the front, side or back; the first foot slides out with the knee bending; as the body pushes up into the air, the second leg catches up with it; they land and the first foot immediately starts to repeat the slide.

Sodium: See salt.

Sousa, John Philip: The American "March King" and composer of the *Stars and Stripes Forever.*

Spices: Ingredients that are used in very small quantities to give an extra special taste to food. They compensate very nicely for a lack of salt when you omit salt. Many have antibiotic powers: onion, garlic, allspice, oregano, thyme, tarragon, cumin, cloves, bay leaf and cayenne pepper. Others are strong antioxidants: oregano, thyme, sage, cumin, rosemary, saffron, turmeric, nutmeg, ginger, cardamom, coriander, basil and tarragon.

Spotting: Looking at one spot as long as possible, without tilting the head; then quickly turning the head while you do a turn; and looking again at the same spot. It promotes sharper turns, better focus, and a better sense of direction while turning and keeps you from getting dizzy.

Stamina: Consists of muscular strength together with endurance.

Static stretch: A slow controlled stretch involving the use of a held position (same as passive stretch).

Stearic acid: A colorless saturated fatty acid found in natural animal products and in some plant foods like chocolate. Unlike most saturated fats, it does not increase cholesterol levels in the blood; liver enzymes change it to unsaturated fat while it is being digested. The calorie count remains the same for all fats and oils.

Step, ball change: Step close step, usually to the front or side, but it can be done to the back also.

Strain: An injury caused by overuse or overexertion.

Strength: The force a muscle produces in one effort.

Stride jumps: Jumps with the feet landing apart, either front-back or out to the sides.

Stride sitting: Legs are apart and out to the sides while sitting.

Supine: Lying on your back.

Syncopation: A shift of accent that occurs when a normally weak beat is stressed in a movement or in a musical composition.

Tai chi: A gentle martial art known to be excellent for improving balance and increasing bone density.

Tarragon: A spice containing potassium.

Teratogenic: Causing malformations of an embryo or fetus when environmental pollutants like PCBs amass in animal tissue.

Terpenoids: Phytochemicals found in whole grains, whole wheat, oats, barley, rye, and brown rice. They may help reduce heart disease and cancer risk.

Theaflavin: An antioxidant found in black tea that may help to reduce LDL and diminish risk of heart attack.

Thiamine: See Vitamin B-1.

Thyme: A spice that resembles Vitamin E in its antioxidant powers.

Trans fats: These will raise the level of bad fats – LDL – and triglycerides, impair arterial flexibility and lower the HDL – good fats in the body – and should be avoided. They form when polyunsaturated fats such as vegetable oils are hydrogenated – a chemical process in which hydrogen atoms are added – and these fats are then solidified to make shortening and some margarines for use in various packaged foods: doughnuts, cakes, crackers, cereals, frozen meals, stick margarine, and fried fast foods, for a longer shelf life. Read the labels on the products to avoid "trans fats" or "hydrogenated fats."

Triglycerides: These are a third type of fat found in the blood. People with a high level of this fat often have higher LDL and lower HDL levels, although triglycerides on their own do not cause the accumulation of fat in the arteries. To lower the triglycerides eat fewer empty calories such as, sugar, white bread and donuts since your body manufactures triglycerides from these high calorie carbohydrates.

Turmeric: A spice with the power to lower insulin and blood sugar levels, but it is not as strong as cinnamon. It is a component of curry powder and contains a very strong antioxidant, curcumin, which blocks the growth of cancer cells and, according to research, may help fight against Alzheimer's and also relieve arthritis and muscle and post operative pain and swelling without the side effects of some pain medications.

Twist (lower torso): The lower torso (hips) twist to the right and to the left from the balls of the feet – the whole area as one – while the upper torso remains stationary.

Twist (upper torso): The upper torso rotates to the right and then to the left while the lower torso remains stationary.

Upstage: The back of the stage. The term dates to the time when stages were slanted and one walked up to go to the back.

Visualization: Forming a clear mental picture of how a position or movement should look, to assist one in its execution.

Vitamins: Organic compounds that are vital to body functions; some can be synthesized in the body and others only in insufficient quantity, even though the necessary amount is small. Some are water soluble – the B group and C; others are not water soluble but are fat soluble – A, D, E and K. Any excess of the fat-soluble ones is stored in the liver, is not easily excreted, and so does not have to be consumed daily. Thus, supplements of these vitamins, or very rich sources such as liver may lead to toxic excesses, especially for

155

pregnant women. Plant sources, carotenes, from which vitamin A can be made, are not as toxic. Water-soluble vitamins, on the other hand, leach into cooking water, are excreted in the urine, a toxic excess rarely happens, and they must be consumed daily for a deficiency not to occur.

Vitamin A or Retinol: A fat soluble nutrient that depends on fat to get to where it is needed, to produce new cells for keeping skin rejuvenated and bones and red blood cells healthy. It is required for normal growth, development and vision. It helps maintain the immune function and protects against oxidation. A shortage of vitamin A can cause night blindness and decreased resistance to infection, slow down growth and lead to disorders of the skin. A diet lacking in fruits and vegetables, based solely on starchy staples and lacking fat, which is necessary for the absorption of vitamin A, is a prime cause of child mortality and blindness in Third World countries. Vitamin A is found in the fatty parts of foods, such as in milk and butter and the tiny quantity of fat in green vegetables like kale, spinach, Swiss chard, and collard, dandelion and turnip greens, as well as in sweet potatoes, pumpkins, and carrots. In vegetables these are known as carotenes, which can be changed to retinol in the wall of the small intestine. Beta-carotenes are strong antioxidants, whereas vitamin A itself is not. Cooking damages neither retinol nor carotenes since they are practically insoluble in water. An excessive amount of vitamin A can cause bones to break down and lead to birth defects. So read the labels on supplements, cereals, and energy bars if you are already taking a multivitamin.

Vitamin B complex: A water soluble group of interrelated vitamins. It reduces stress, boosts your mood, aids in red blood cell production, and helps your body turn food into energy. It is not absorbed from food as readily as from supplements and enriched foods. An extended shortage of a particular vitamin can affect the health; however, the body has enough set aside to enable it to deal with differences from one day to the next. Deficiencies of vitamin B complex can affect appetite, growth, development, and general health, as well as cause such diseases as pellagra and beriberi.

Vitamin B-1 – Thiamine: It is water soluble, indispensable for the utilization of carbohydrates by living cells, maintains the nervous system, heart and muscle tissue. It is found in meat, the bran coat of grains, fortified bread and cereals, enriched flour, and yeast. It is not stored in the body so a constant supply is needed. A deficiency can cause loss of appetite, fatigue, and if severe, beriberi.

Vitamin B-2 – Riboflavin: A nutrient that is concerned with the body's energy-releasing mechanism, and also promotes repair of tissue, healthy skin, hair and nails. It is found in liver, dairy, eggs, yeast, whole grain bread, fortified cereals, spinach, sweet potatoes and mushrooms. While only slightly soluble in water, it is sensitive to light, but not to heat. When eaten it is stored for a short time in the liver. Deficiency may cause hypersensitivity to light and cracks at the corners of the mouth.

Vitamin B-3 – Niacin: A nutrient that is found in fruits, vegetables, eggs, milk, enriched breads and fortified cereals, fish, poultry and meat. The amino acid tryptophan found in high protein foods is another source, since it can be converted to niacin. This vitamin helps to change carbohydrates into energy and promotes healthy digestive and nervous systems. Losses in cooking are minor. Severe deficiency leads to pellagra, characterized by mental disorder, dermatitis, and diarrhea.

Vitamin B-5 or Panthotenic acid: It is found in fruits, vegetables, grains, yogurt, meat and fish. It maintains adrenal hormones and is concerned with energy metabolism. It is excellent for relieving allergies and protecting the body from stress. A deficiency may cause leg cramps and insomnia.

Vitamin B-6 or Pyridoxine: This nutrient is necessary for protein metabolism, for the immune function and the nervous system. It is also concerned in the synthesis of red blood cells and hormones and helps control blood glucose. It is found in pork, poultry, fish, shellfish, milk, beans, peas, potatoes, Brussels sprouts, bananas, whole grains, pistachios, chestnuts, prunes, and avocados. A deficiency may cause insomnia.

Vitamin B-9: See Folate (Folic acid, or folacin).

Vitamin B-12 – Cobalamin: A nutrient found in meats, dairy products, eggs, liver, fish, and fortified cereals, and is needed for building red blood cells, for maintaining nerve cells and for the synthesis of RNA and DNA. The liver is able to store large amounts of B-12. The absorption and digestive process for B-12 is very complicated; since the process may be incomplete in those over 50 years of age, they are often recommended to take supplements (such as one multivitamin) that are more readily absorbed. Severe deficiency can cause memory loss, confusion, weakening and tingling in the limbs, hallucinations and listlessness, pernicious anemia as well as hearing impairment. People with these symptoms may be misdiagnosed as having Alzheimer's or as "getting old". Strict vegetarians who eat no eggs or dairy foods may have a deficiency.

Vitamin C – Ascorbic Acid: is a highly water soluble antioxidant (in the case of canned foods, much of it will go into the liquid, which should be used). It is vital in the production of collagen, helps in healing wounds, cuts and bruises, keeps blood vessels strong, protects the body against free radicals, heart disease, cancer and infection, helps other vitamins work, and is important for the body's absorption of iron; it strengthens bones, cartilage and skin. An adequate supply of vitamin C prevents scurvy. It is found in citrus fruits, berries, guava, kiwi, mango, papaya, and in numerous vegetables, such as tomatoes, potatoes, sweet potatoes, bell peppers, kale, collard greens, Swiss chard, and in the cabbage family: broccoli, Brussels sprouts, and cauliflower. Food will lose less of its vitamin C content when it is cooked if it is placed in a small amount of boiling water instead of cold water.

Vitamin D – Calciferol: "The sunlight vitamin" is a fat-soluble vitamin; it works in conjunction with calcium and magnesium to preserve bone structure and prevent osteoporosis. It is found in fortified milk, dairy foods, egg yolks, herring, halibut, sardines, eel, mackerel, salmon, and liver. As cholecalciferol it is obtained from the action of sunlight on animal skin, while ergocalciferol is the vitamin D found in small amounts in dark green leafy vegetables. It is needed for maximum calcium absorption and has been connected with fewer bone fractures in those over 65 years. A deficiency causes rickets in the young, caused by lack of calcium, sunlight or vitamin D.

Vitamin E – Alpha-tocopherol: A fat soluble vitamin valuable in keeping skin and blood cells healthy and fighting heart disease by inhibiting the activity of free radicals. It is found in sweet potatoes, nuts, whole grains, barley, wheat germ, green leafy vegetables, avocado, asparagus and vegetable oils. People who have high levels of vitamin E in their diets have less likelihood of getting Alzheimer's. Vitamin E also assists in preventing macular degeneration, cataracts and in enhancing immunity.

Vitamin K: It is essential for the clotting of blood so that wounds heal more rapidly, and it also lowers the risk of hip fractures from osteoporosis by helping to maintain bone density. Spinach is a rich source of vitamin K. The body can create a form of vitamin K – menaquinone – as well as that obtained from food – phylloquinone. Deficiency usually only occurs in newborn, premature infants.

Water: It is essential to the body; it carries fuel to the muscles, lubricates the joints, and helps keep the body cool through sweat. Lack of it causes fatigue and causes kidney problems.

Water soluble vitamins: The vitamins that are soluble in water are B and C.

Weight training: This training involves the use of either free weights or machines.

Working leg: The leg that does all the movement, as opposed to the standing leg.

Yoga: A workout that combines controlled deep breathing and concentration with stretching and strengthening postures and progressing at your own pace.

Zeaxanthin: An antioxidant in the carotenoid family, found in yellow/green vegetables: corn, squash, avocado, green peas, turnip greens, collards, spinach, honeydew and also in red bell peppers. Together with the antioxidant lutein it reduces the risk of macular degeneration and cataracts in the eyes

Zinc: A mineral involved with growth, reproductive organs, taste perception, wound healing, preventing infection, and strengthening immunity. It is vital for the activity of enzymes involved with energy changes and protein formation. It is found in beef, lamb, pork, eggs, liver, shellfish, oysters, whole grains, and legumes. Excess can cause gastrointestinal irritation, copper deficiency and impaired immune function.

DISCOGRAPHY

"Bo Diddley"

"Shimmele, Shimmele Ko Ko Bop"

"Ultra Dance Various" – RCA Victor #AFL 1-5322

Billboards "Top Latin Hits"

"Love for Three Oranges" from *Romeo and Juliet* – by Sergei Prokofiev

"Yakety Axe" – arranged by Chet Atkins for RCA Victor

"Let's Go" – Wang Chung

"Stars and Stripes Forever" – by John Philip Sousa

"Dancin' in the Dark" – Bruce Springsteen

"Clap Yo' Hands"

"O, Them Golden Slippers"

"West Side Story" by Leonard Bernstein

"Puff the Magic Dragon" – Peter, Paul and Mary

"Starlight Express" – Broadway musical

"Gypsy" – by Stephen Sondheim

"The People on the Bus"

"My Favorite Things" from Rodgers and Hammerstein's *Sound of Music*

"It's a Raggy Waltz" – Dave Brubeck Quartet

Waltz of your choice by Johann Strauss

"When I Think of You" – Janet Jackson

"I Didn't Mean to Turn You On" – Robert Palmer

"Whole Lot-ta Shakin' Goin' On" – Jerry Lee Lewis, 1957

Billboards "Top Dance Hits" (of any year since 1974)

"Jingle Bells" – arranged by Duke Ellington

"One O'Clock Boogie" – Count Basie

"Supernatural" – Santana

"Golden Age Polka" – by Shostakovitch

"Brandenburg Concertos" – by Johann Sebastian Bach

Modern Jazz Quartet – with Milt Jackson on Vibraphone and John Lewis on piano

"Swingin' Them Jingle Bells" – arranged by Fats Waller

"Quintet in A, Opus 114, 'The Trout', 4th movement" – by Franz Schubert

Selections from musicals – "Carousel", "Oklahoma", "Cats", "On the Town"

BIBLIOGRAPHY

COOKING

American Heart Association. *American Heart Association One Dish Meals: over 200 all-new, all-in-one recipes.* NY: Clarkson Potter, 2003.

American Heart Association. *The American Heart Association Quick and Easy Cookbook: More Than 200 Healthful Recipes You Can Make In Minutes.* NY: Crown Publishing Group, 2001.

American Heart Association. *The New American Heart Association Cookbook,* 25th Anniversary Edition. NY: Times Books, Random House, 1998.

Bauer, Joy, M.S., R.D., C.D.N. *Cooking With Joy.* NY: St. Martin's Press, 2004.

Brody, Jane. *Jane Brody's Good Food Gourmet.* NY: W.W. Norton & Company, 1990.

Cooper, Leslie L. *Low-Fat Living Cookbook.* Emmaus, PA: Rodale Press, Inc., distributed by St Martin's Press, 1998.

Dieckmann, Jane Marsh. *Low Fat One-Dish Meals from around the World.* Freedom, CA: The Crossing Press, 1993.

Giedt, Frances Towner. *Low-Carb Quick & Easy.* NY: HPBooks, Published by The Berkley Publishing Group, a division of Penguin Group, 2004.

Hensrud, Donald, Jennifer Nelson, Cheryl Farberg and Maureen Callahan. *The New Mayo Clinic Cookbook, Eating Well for Better Health.* Menlo Park, CA: Oxmoor House, 2004.

Jenkins, Nancy Harmon. *The Mediterranean Diet Cookbook, A Delicious Alternative for Lifelong Health.* NY: Bantam Books, 1994.

Jones, Jeanne. *Canyon Ranch Cooking: Bringing the Spa Home.* NY, NY: HarperCollins Publishers, Inc., 1998.

Ragone, RD, Regina. "Family Table – Bliss in a Bowl." *Prevention,* October, 2003, Pgs. 148-156A.

Sailac, Alain, Ed. *French Culinary Institute Salute to Healthy Cooking: from America's Foremost French Chefs.* Emmaus, PA: Rodale Press, (distributed by St. Martin's Press), 1998.

Tribole, Evelyn, M.S., R.D. *More Healthy Homestyle Cooking.* NY: Rodale Press, distributed by St. Martin's Press, 2000.

University of California at Berkeley and the Editors of the Wellness Cooking School. *The Wellness Lowfat Cookbook.* NY: Rebus Inc. Publishers (distributed by Random House), 2003.

DANCE AND MOVEMENT

Andreu, Helene. *Aerobic Razzmatazz: 12 Workouts by 12 Minutes Each.* Bloomington, IN.: 1st Books Library (now AuthorHouse), 2000.

Andreu, Helene. *Jazz Dance, An Adult Beginner's Guide.* Englewood Cliffs, NJ: Prentice Hall, Inc., 1983.

Andreu, Helene. *Jazz Dance Styles and Steps for Fun.* Bloomington, IN.: 1st Books Library (now AuthorHouse), 2003.

Audy, Robert. *Tap Dancing – How to Teach Yourself.* NY: Random House, 1976.

Blom, Lynne Anne and I. Tarin Chaplin. *The Moment of Movement.* Pittsburgh, PA: The University of Pittsburgh Press, 1988.

Cheney, Gay. *Basic Concepts in Modern Dance, A Creative Approach*, 3rd Edition. Pennington, NJ: A Dance Horizons Book, Princeton Book Company, Publishers, 1989.

Hughes, Russell Meriweather. *The Gesture Language of the Hindu Dance / La Meri.* NY: Arno Press, 1979.

Moss, Dena Simone and Allison Kyle Leopold. *The Joffrey Ballet School's Ballet-Fit.* NY: St. Martin's Griffen, 1988.

Nagrin, Daniel. *How to Dance Forever: Surviving Against the Odds.* NY: William Morrow, 1988.

Sherbon, Elizabeth. *On the Count of One: Modern Dance Methods.* Palo Alto, CA: Mayfield Publishing Co., 1975.

Shipley, Glenn. *Modern Tap Dictionary.* Los Angeles, CA: Action Marketing Group, 1976.

Shook, Karel. *Elements of Classical Ballet Technique, as practiced in the school of the Dance Theatre of Harlem.* NY: Dance Horizons, 1977.

Stephenson, Richard, M. and Joseph Iaccarino. *The Complete Book of Ballroom Dancing.* NY: Doubleday, 1992.

Stuart, Muriel. *The Classical Ballet: Technique and Terminology.* NY: Knopf, 1962.

Vaganova, Agrippina. *Fundamentals of the Class Dance.* NY: Dover, 1971.

FITNESS

Alzheimer's Research Review. Clarksburg, MD: Alzheimer's Disease Research, a program of the American Health Assistance Foundation, Quarterly, 2000-2004.

"America's Obesity Crisis." *Time Magazine,* June 7, 2004, Pgs. 57-113.

American Heart Association. *Fitting In Fitness.* NY: Times Books (a division of Random House), 1997.

Barry, Suzanne. *Basic Pilates.* NY: Barnes and Noble, Inc., 2004.

Beach, Nancy. "The New Science of Fitness." *The New York Times,* April 16, 1978.

Brody, Jane. "Personal Health." *The New York Times,* 1984-2004.

Brooklyn Women's Health. Office of Institutional Advancement, SUNY Downstate Medical Center, Brooklyn, NY, Spring 2003.

Christensen, Alice, founder American Yoga Assn. *The American Yoga Association's Beginner's Manual.* NY: A Fireside Book, published by Simon & Schuster, 2002.

Consumer Reports on Health. Yonkers, N.Y.: Consumers Union, 2001-2004, Monthly.

Department of Health and Human Services. *Healthy People 2000.* Boston: Jones and Bartlett Publishers, Inc., 1992.

Elliot, D. L. and Goldberg, L. "Nutrition and exercise." *Medical Clinics of North America, 69, 71-8,* 1985.

Fitness Magazine Editors with Karen Andos. *The Complete Book of Fitness.* NY, NY: Three Rivers Press, 1999.

For Your Information (An AARP Health Care Options Publication). Washington, DC: AARP, 2001-2003.

Franks, B. Don, Ph.D., Edward T. Howley, Ph.D. and Yuruk Iyriboz, M.D. *The Health Fitness Handbook.* Champaign, IL: Human Kinetics, 1999.

Garrow, J S. "The management of obesity, another view." *International Journal of Obesity,* 16 (suppl. 2), S59-S63, 1992.

Healthy Decisions. Brooklyn, NY: Lutheran Medical Center, 2001-2003.

Kent, Allegra with James and Constance Camner. *The Dancer's Body Book.* NY: William Morrow, 1984.

Kraftsow, Gary. *Yoga For Transformation.* NY: Penguin Compass, 2002.

Lindsay, Ruth, Billie J. Jones and Ada Van Whitley. *Body Mechanics.* William C Brown and Co., 1974.

Maisel, Edward. *Tai Chi for Health.* NY: Barnes and Noble, Inc., 1999.

"Manage Stress, Manage Illness, A Special Report." *USA Weekend (together with Men's Health),* May 28-30, 2004, Pgs. 6-14.

New York Medical Press. Medical Society of the State of New York, 2003.

Shafarman, Steven. *Awareness Heals – The Feldenkrais Method for Dynamic Health.* NY: Perseus Books at HarperCollins Publishers, 1997.

Spilner, Maggie, Walking Editor, Prevention Magazine. *Prevention's Complete Book of Walking – Everything You Need to Know to Walk Your Way to Better Health.* NY: Rodale, Inc., 2000.

Thomas, David Q., Ph.D. and Nicki E. Rippee, Ph.D. *Is Your Aerobics Class Killing You?* Chicago, IL: a cappella books/Chicago Review Press, Inc., 1992.

University of California, Berkeley. The Wellness Encyclopedia, The Comprehensive Family Resource for Safeguarding Health and Preventing Illness. Boston, : Houghton Mifflin Company, 1991.

Vincent, L. M., M.D. *The Dancer's Book of Health.* Mission, KS: Sheed Andrews and McMeel, Inc., a subsidiary of Universal Press Syndicate, 1978.

Wellness Letter, The Newsletter of Nutrition, Fitness and Self-Care. University of California, Berkeley, CA, 2000-2005.

NUTRITION

Beerbower, Karen, R. D. *Setting Places.* Maitland, FL: Nutritional Guidance, Inc., 2000.

"Carbohydrates." *Harvard School of Public Health.* http://www.hsph.harvard.edu/ nutritionsource/carbohydrates.html, Feb. 19, 2004.

Carper, Jean. "Eat Smart." *USA Weekend,* a Division of Gannett Co. Inc., 2001-2004.

Carper, Jean. *Food – Your Miracle Medicine.* NY: HarperCollins, 1993.

Diplock, A. T., "Antioxidant and Disease Prevention: An overview." *American Journal of Clinical Nutrition* 53, 189S-193S, 1991.

Fox, Brian A. and Allan G. Cameron. *Food Science, Nutrition and Health,* Sixth Edition. London: Edward Arnold, a member of Hodder Headline Group, 1995.

Gittleman, Ann Louise, L. S., C.N.S. *Get The Salt Out, 501 Simple Ways to Cut The Salt Out of Your Diet.* NY: Crown Trade Paperbacks, 1996.

Gregor, J. L. "Dietary Supplement Use: Consumer Characteristics and Interests." *The Journal of Nutrition,* Vol. 131, No. 4S. April 2001, Pgs. 1339S-1343S.

Harris, M. B. "Eating habits, restraint, knowledge and attitude toward obesity." *International Journal of Obesity,* 7, 271-286, 1983.

"Healthy Eating Pyramid." *Harvard School of Public Health,* http://www.hsph.harvard.edu/ nutritionsource/pyramids.html, 2/19/04.

Heber, David, Dr. with Susan Bowerman. *What Color Is Your Diet?* New York, N.Y.: Regan Books, an imprint of HarperCollins Publishers, Inc., 2001.

Hegsted, D. M. "Calcium and osteoporosis." *Journal of Nutrition,* 116, 2316-231, 1986.

Joseph, James, Ph.D., Dr. Daniel A. Nadeau and Anne Underwood. *The Color Code – A Revolutionary Eating Plan for Optimum Health.* NY: Hyperion, 2002.

Knekt, P., J. Kumpulainen, R. Jarvinen, M. Heliovaara, A. Reunanen, T. Hakulinen and A. Aromaa. "Flavonoid intake and risk of chronic diseases." *The American Journal of Clinical Nutrition,* Vol. 76, No.3, Sept. 2002, Pgs. 560-568.

Marsh, A. G., T.V. Sanchez, O. Michelsen, F.L. Chaffee, and S.M. Fagal. "Vegetarian lifestyle and bone mineral density." *American Journal of Clinical Nutrition,* 48, 837-841, 1988.

Pritikin, Robert. *The Pritikin Weight Loss Breakthrough, Five Easy Steps to Outsmart Your Fat Instinct,* NY: A Dutton Book, Published by the Penguin Group, 1998.

"Protein." *Harvard School of Public Health.* http://www.hsph.harvard.edu/nutritionsource/ protein.html, February 19, 2004.

Sears, Barry, Ph. D. *A Week in the Zone.* NY: Harper Collins Publishers, Inc., 2000.

Simopoulos, Artemis P. "The Mediterranean Diets: What Is So Special About the Diet of Greece? The Scientific Evidence." *Journal of Nutrition,* Nov. 2001, Supplement, Vol. 13, No. 11S, Pg. 30655.

Steinmetz, K. A. "Vegetables, fruit and cancer prevention: a review." *Journal of the American Dietetic Association,* 96 (10):1027-39, 1996.

Tucker, K. L., H. Chen, M.T. Hannan, L.A. Cupples, P.W.F. Wilson, D. Felson, and D. P. Kiel. "Bone mineral density and dietary patterns in older adults: the. Framingham Osteoporosis Study." *The American Journal of Clinical Nutrition,* Vol. 76, No.1, July 2002, Pgs. 245-252.

Webb, Geoffrey P. BSc, MSc, PhD. *Nutrition, A Health Promotion Approach.* London: Arnold, A member of the Hodder Headline Group, 1995.

Wollin, Stephanie D. and Peter J. H. Jones. "Alcohol, Red Wine and Cardiovascular Disease." *The Journal of Nutrition,* No. 131 (4-6), April-June 2001, Pgs. 1401-1404.

Yeager, Selene and the Editors of Prevention. *Prevention's New Foods for Healing.* Emmaus, PA: Rodale Press Inc., distributed by St Martin's Press, 1998.

"Your Health – What's Worse Than Sugar?" *AARP Bulletin,* April 2004.

INDEX

Printed in the United States
129822LV00001B/9/A

9 781425 927585